Endorsements

If you want to ignite your imagination of courageous and creative post-Christendom missionary thought and action in Canada, read *Text & Context*. This stimulating collection of essays and first-person narratives offers compelling theological, cultural, contextual, and practical ideas. It is grounded in a missional spirituality toward contextualization and discipleship, and packed with lucid questions and concrete examples. *Text & Context* is a lively resource that paints colorful pictures of what organic, process and people oriented, missional communities and church plants can look like in different settings. I vigorously recommend it.

Roger Helland, DMin
District Coach of the Baptist General Conference in Alberta
Author of *Magnificent Surrender* (Wipf & Stock, 2012), co-author of *Missional Spirituality* (IVP, 2011).

In a world where we find ourselves facing constantly new and rapidly changing realities, in post Christendom urban Canada where Christianity is something that many have been inoculated against, we need stories which can help us begin to imagine new possibilities. The power of *Text & Context* is that it has done just that. It is the range and diversity of the book which is its strength. None of the church plants are presented as models to be applied, but rather, they are given to us, like the Kingdom parables, as narratives to help us see things differently. When read as something to fire imagination, not to outline a blueprint, this book has the capacity to serve as a profound gift.

Donald Goertz
Associate Professor of Church History
Director of the MDiv. In Ministry
Tyndale University College and Seminary

TEXT
& CONTEXT

Church Planting in Canada in Post-Christendom

Other books by Leonard Hjalmarson

No Home Like Place: A Theology of Place. (forthcoming)
The Missional Church Fieldbook (Portland: Urban Loft Publishers, 2013).
Missional Spirituality: Embodying God's Love from the Inside Out (Downers Grove: IVP, 2011).
An Emerging Dictionary for the Gospel and Culture: A Conversation from Augustine to Zizek (Eugene: Resource Publications, 2010).

TEXT & CONTEXT

Church Planting in Canada in Post-Christendom

Edited by Leonard Hjalmarson

Urban Loft Publishers | Portland, Oregon

Urban Loft Publishers
2034 NE 40th Avenue #414
Portland, OR 97212
www.theurbanloft.org

ISBN-13: 978-1492721246
ISBN-10: 1492721247

Made in the U.S.A.

Acknowledgements

In 2007, growing out of a conversation on the RESONATE mailing list, Brent Toderash and I began gathering contributors from across the country who had a story to tell in the midst of an adventure they were living: church planting in a post-Christendom culture. This book revisits and updates many of those stories and adds five new ones to the mix.

Special thanks to Sean Benesh of Urban Loft Publishers, who encouraged this fresh look at the church on mission amidst Canada's accelerating pluralism.

Thanks also to Dan Steigerwald for permission to reprint his essay on the top challenges facing urban missionaries in this unique social location.

Thanks to Dave Fitch for allowing us to reprint his fine essay. A traveler who moves between Canada and the United States, Dave is a careful theological thinker as well as a church planter. His recent book with Geoff Holsclaw, *Prodigal Christianity*, maps a middle ground between the Neo-Reformed and Emergent movements.

Finally, thanks to Bob Roxburgh for his friendship on this journey, and to Scott Hagley of FORGE Canada for his reflections and challenge to kingdom entrepreneurs in the Afterword. We do indeed need both risk and reflection!

May this work prove even more engaging than the first, and may it shine a little more light on those intrepid Kingdom adventurers we call "church planters."

Contents

Then, suddenly, out of the strange silence and strange motion there came a tremendous roar.

The Eagle Rock on the south wall, about a half a mile up the valley, gave way and I saw it falling in thousands of ... great boulders.

As soon as those rock avalanches fell, the streams began to sing new songs ... by what at first sigh seemed pure confounded confusion and ruin, the landscapes were enriched.

John Muir, The Earthquake

Foreword

Bob Roxburgh

The contributors to this book have done Canadian church planters a tremendous service. From the introductory chapters through to the stories of various plants/missional communities to the final chapter outlining church planting principles, this is such a practical and hopeful volume!

In the Introduction, Len Hjalmarson points out the difficulties of planting in the contemporary Canadian culture with its huge shifts and its marginalization of traditional Christianity. It doesn't sound good: but it may not be bad news, after all, for as in the Babylonian Captivity there is much one can relearn about God, his mission, and the life of a faith community in his Kingdom. It is an opportunity for God's people to gain a fresh vision of God and what he is up to. Here we can rediscover that the work of the Kingdom goes beyond "church-work."

In our current context, it is sometimes difficult to get "emergents" talking to "missional" people, and either of these groups talking to people in the traditional church setting. Yet wherever we find ourselves on Stuart Murray's spectrum, whether an "inherited church" or an "emerging church," we all face the same issues and all have new opportunities in this day and age. Here's hoping this book contributes to deeper conversation and insight, and opens new doors for collaboration.

These Canadian stories show us how this is working out in a variety of contexts, across a very wide geographic expanse. All across Canada, communities are discovering afresh what God is up to in the present culture and how we can best connect with the work of his Kingdom to form genuine missionary communities. They are all discovering that Church is not where you go but where we live. There is so much being learned in connecting with both the un-churched and de-churched (people who have left for a variety of reasons, yet who continue on some kind of spiritual journey).

This superb volume goes on to describe how various church planters are trying to deal with the issues that both Hjalmarson and Fitch raise so well in the introductory chapters. Fitch points out that it is a whole new ballgame, and that it therefore takes a whole new approach (in leadership, for example), and that we must see ourselves as cultivating a garden rather than running an organisation or directing a church per se. This shift away from management paradigms to something more organic is helpful, and pushes us toward the adaptive need.

The stories from across Canada reveal how different groups are engaging in the new culture and adapting to their context while remaining faithful to the gospel. The nuances and variations are there, but the principle is common, namely that of empowering others. People these days are being cultivated more than directed or informed. Yet the paradigm has shifted from church growth to spiritual formation, and is also gradually shifting away from the individual to the community, the "hermeneutic of the gospel," as Lesslie Newbigin articulated so well.

This recovery of diversity, and the move to "create" and not clone, bodes well for the future of the Christian movement in Canada. While big churches will remain part of the landscape for some time to come, the experiments that are taking root are mostly small and contextual. This means less need to import models from elsewhere (usually the U.S.A.) and may also mean that Canadians will soon become a resource for our neighbours to the south, reversing what up to now was the expected flow. Creativity is by necessity diverse and contextual, and the testimonies from across this vast land of ours are coming from diverse traditions—ranging from Vineyard to Anglican and to everything in between. We really are learning from one another and experimenting together into the future. As Mark Scandrette points out in *The Gospel After Christendom*, "most of our knowledge of God is gained through risk."[1]

Indeed, *Text & Context* shares much with the ethos of that great book, though Bolger's collection ranges more widely in representing a worldwide movement. But like Bolger, *Text & Context* shows us reality in the stories of struggles and pain, as well as the fruitfulness that comes from listening to the Spirit where God has placed us. The stories here remind us that we are not dealing with novelty or change for the sake of change, but the power of incarnational mission and the need to recover a community hermeneutic: listening to the Lord and the culture together in the light of the Scriptures.

My personal encouragement is that so many of the dreams promised to the "old" leaders in Acts 2 (I am in my 70s) are being fulfilled and expressed in these stories. and not just as anecdotes but as a working out of excellent reflection on the Scriptures. I am pleased that no one presumes to offer the method or approach. On the contrary, these are all expressions of how communities are seeing God at work and what is happening to his disciples as they catch *missio Dei*.

Just as our culture keeps going through discontinuous change, so these testimonies of faith communities that remain open to what they must do or change to keep in step with the Spirit. I closed the book, full of hope, wishing I was 35 years old again.

About Bob Roxburgh

Bob Roxburgh does church consulting in his retirement after 50 years of creative pastoral ministries in UK, USA and Canada. He was adjunct professor at various seminaries in all three countries and lectured worldwide on the renewal of the Church. His book *Renewal Down To Earth* described a balanced approach to the charismatic renewal existing in the UK in the 80s. He resides in Kelowna, BC with his wife Brenda.

Bibliography

Scandrette, Mark. "The Jesus Dojo." In *The Gospel After Christendom: New Voices, New Cultures, New Expressions*, edited by Roger K. Bolger. Grand Rapids: Baker Academic, 2012. Kindle edition.

---

1 Scandrette, "The Jesus Dojo." Kindle edition.

Introduction

Post-Christendom and Adaptive Challenge
Leonard Hjalmarson

In 1901, 37 percent of Canadians lived in urban areas. By 2006, that figure had risen to 80 percent. Two-thirds of Canadians now live within 33 urban centers with populations of more than 100,000.[1]

In Canada, prior to 1971, one percent of Canadians reported no religious affiliation. In the 2012 national Census, that figure had climbed to 24 percent for adults and 32 percent for teens, suggesting this number will continue to trend upward. The rate is highest in British Columbia, the "California" of Canada, with 44 percent of adults and teens declaring no religious affiliation. Even in the Fraser Valley, BC's "Bible Belt," 30 percent reported no religious preference.[2]

We live in a time of tremendous shaking. Recent surveys by the Barna Group[3] and books such as *You Lost Me*[4] indicate that more and more believers are leaving the Church, and many others don't attend any regular gathering of believers. Diana Butler Bass asks, "What is causing the erosion of Christianity in North America? Most North Americans look at Christianity – especially as embodied in religious institutions – and find it wanting ... Although young North Americans express deep longings for a loving, just, and peaceful world, they don't find an equal

17

passion for transforming society in meaningful ways in most congregations."[5] Yet at the same time, there is a growing spiritual hunger: a hunger for transcendence, a hunger for significant relationships, and a hunger to connect with meaning. Reggie McNeal says of so-called "secular" culture that it is now "more spiritual than the church culture."[6]

There have been other such times in history, when cultural shift left the Church on shaky ground because it was wedded to a world that was passing away. The Reformation, starting in the early days of the Enlightenment, was a response to such conditions. The Old Testament records similar transitions, as explored by scholars such as Walter Brueggemann.

Living in Exile

In Cadences of Home[7] Brueggemann documents the first diaspora when Israel went into exile, living far from Jerusalem in Babylon. He describes this theologically as the movement "from Temple to text," and argues that while there was a loss of political freedom this was a time of tremendous theological creativity: a rediscovery of the freedom of God and a re-appropriation of faith and hope. Could it be that when everything is shaken God invites us to embrace a new level of dependence and a renewed faith?

Other scholars from other disciplines are asking that question. In *The Upside of Down*, for example, Thomas Homer-Dixon writes, "We can get ready in advance to turn to our advantage any breakdown that does occur ... We can boost the chances that it will lead to renewal by being well prepared, nimble and smart and by learning to recognize its many warning signs."[8] Elsewhere he coins a word for the process of renewal that comes through breakdown: *catagenesis*. *Catagenesis* describes a process that results when complex adaptive systems adapt to new conditions. The contributors to this project are all confident that the Church will survive into the future in some form, and who are not allied to structures but rather to Jesus. Wine grows old, and wineskins will change, but the Spirit who indwells the Body is the unchanging Lord.[9]

At the same time, we are rooted in our culture. We sense the challenge of transition, the threat to our own equilibrium, and more deeply, to our sense of identity as church and ministry leaders. We are accustomed to managing problems and comforting people: suddenly the problems are so unique that we have no ready answers.[10] That isn't easy to admit. Moreover, at some level we fear the unknown and the pain of transition. Christendom, the legacy of Constantine and of the Enlightenment, gave us a Church of the center, a Church allied with the dominant forms of economic, intellectual, cultural and social life. We have been wealthy and comfortable, and sometimes, we thought, "in need of nothing." The current shaking exposes our insecurity, our need for comfort, and at times, our compromise and lack of faith.

We should note at the outset, as Nathan Colquohoun reminds us, that there is no language of church planting in the New Testament. That language, and the modalities that accompanied it, was developed in a Christendom context, when mission was understood as the possession of the Church, and when the boundaries between Church and kingdom were blurred. We use the language of "church planting" here as a legacy: a limited, colonial, and Western frame of imagination that is fading away in favor of the *missio Dei*.[11]

Taxonomy: Inherited versus Emerging

In this volume we explore the Canadian cultural landscape and the intersection of faith and culture through the lenses of two kinds of practitioners: church planters and mentors/leadership coaches. It's helpful to begin with a mental map, a taxonomy. We'll use two. First a frame offered by Stuart Murray in *Church After Christendom*, distinguishing between "inherited" and "emerging" churches,[12] a more helpful framework than emerging versus institutional, and much more fluid than the often advanced dichotomy of organic versus organized. Second, an organizational lens borrowed from Drew Goodmanson that diagrams the polarity of attractional and incarnational. Really this is a missiological/contextual frame that also works readily as a lens for examining the shifting relationship of the local church in her context. That context was once Christendom; it is rapidly becoming post-Christendom (I am thinking here of the quip, "The future is already here; it just isn't evenly distributed.") First, we consider Stuart Murray and his taxonomy.

Murray notes that every church is "inherited" to some degree, then suggests three types of emergence, some of which are closer than others to inheritance.

- churches emerging from inherited church through processes of renewal and transformation. The outcome is not another church, but a church more or less radically different from the past in structure, ethos, style, focus or activity.
- churches emerging out of inherited church through processes of community engagement, liturgical exploration, church planting or missiological reflection. The outcome is a new, or embryonic church, that becomes more or less autonomous.
- churches emerging within a particular context without the shaping influence of or significant connection to inherited church. The outcome is a new church, which may be more or less radical, that will need to build links with other churches.

Murray calls for open conversations between various groups rather than formal consultation. We need to hear the stories as we attempt to reengage our culture, thus becoming a learning community.[13] He offers Peter with the Jerusalem church in Acts 11 as a paradigm for conversation.[14] The urban missionaries and mentors/coaches who tell their stories in these pages are all ecclesial workers, in relation at some level to the larger story of which they are a local and temporal expression. Their perspective, on the other hand, is unique because they stand in a new social location. By nature they are learners, and by their own admission, they are discovering new questions as they journey.

Attractional or Incarnational?

The second taxonomy is offered by Goodmanson in his paper, "Triperspectival Ecclesiology."[15] That five dollar combination is more complicated that it sounds. Goodmanson's intention was to look at the shape of the primary gatherings for three types of Christian communities: the corporate celebration (Christendom, attractional mode); the missional community (existential, home group mode); the tribal encounter, missionary mode (out in the culture, often a neutral "third place" venue). The further to the right on this diagram, the less structured and smaller the gathering, and shading from the center to the right, the more intentionally the gathering will include non-believers.

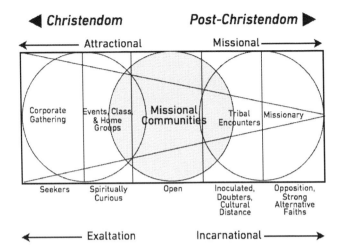

One of the things I like about this diagram is that it neatly places "missional communities" as a middle ground between the attractional and missional/incarnational modes.[16] That's helpful, because missional communities do gather and are attractive. Missional communities exist in the same rhythm that exists in the life of the Trinity: inward in love, outward in mission. The overflowing love of life in community results in mission.

When I first saw this diagram, I realized that it also worked to describe the shifting reality of the Church in culture, thus Christendom pushing to the left, and post-Christendom to the right. Goodmanson is doing a lot with this diagram, as you can see by his tracking the nature of the seeker along the bottom. A similar shift could be diagrammed for leadership models – participation and decentralization are the watchwords in postmodern culture.[17]

Any medical student knows that the proper treatment is dependent on an accurate diagnosis. A plethora of books, articles and dissertations are attempting to help us exegete our culture.[18] At the same time observers are putting a variety of fresh expressions under the spotlight, as evidenced by their various books and papers.[19] If Thomas Homer-

Dixon is right that synergistic energy can result in *catagenesis* in complex systems, we may be observing the emergence of conditions that will engender a new storm system for change.[20]

All of us in this strange new social location are asking new questions about the nature of God and His mission. As Phyllis Tickle points out, with major cultural upheaval all the big questions are up for grabs.[21] The primary one is this: who has (where is) the authority? Two related questions then follow: what does it mean to be truly human? What is the relation of all religions to one another? These questions are below the surface in many discussions I've engaged in the past five years. A renewed interest in theology and Christology surfaces through all these questions, and a reengagement with Trinitarian foundations is at the core of the anthropological question.

Re-Entering Our Neighborhoods

Reg McNeal writes that, "The first Reformation was about freeing the church. The new Reformation is about freeing God's people from the church (the institution). The original Reformation decentralized the church. The new Reformation decentralizes ministry. The former Reformation occurred when clergy were no longer willing to take marching orders from the Pope. The current Reformation finds church members no longer willing for clergy to script their personal spiritual ministry journey. The last Reformation moved the church closer to home. The new Reformation is moving the church closer to the world."[22]

We worship the child born in Bethlehem. God showed up in Israel in a way no one expected. He simply did not fit the Messianic expectations of the Jews. He arrived to ordinary people in an obscure place, in a troubled province on the outskirts of the Roman Empire. He practiced life as a Jew and worked as a carpenter. Those who should have seen saw nothing, while those called "blind" saw clearly.

The great hunger in our age is for belonging. We long for a place where we are rooted, and where we truly belong. At the same time, under the influence of false eschatologies, we wonder if the call to come home will carry us out of this world. This split in our psyche is common in Western churches. Theologians like N. T. Wright (*Surprised by Hope*) and James K. A. Smith (*Desiring the Kingdom*) are helping us move away from this unbiblical dualism. Still others are recovering biblical grounding with the practice of place[23] through the lens of neighbourhood and parish.[24]

In *Christianity for the Rest of Us* Diana Butler Bass describes the recovery of the village church or "parish." How does she use this old word, an expression of the intersection of church and place?[25] The practice of parish was that a local church served its community. The priest or pastor, and the core laypeople who called their parish home, were intimately connected with the life of the neighbourhood. Butler Bass describes the recovery of the parish concept: centered around God's house, the church, offering hospitality for pilgrims in a strange land.[26]

The parish does not exist in the dualistic, insulated and protective mode common to Western evangelical churches: it makes the concerns of the village its own concerns. Neither does it exist in the individualistic conversion mode of the typical evangelical church: its goal is less the conversion of individuals, though this is a good thing, and more the transformation of the village.[27] Michael Northcott connects the story of the parish church to the hope for community-based ecological politics.[28] (You'll hear echoes of these goals in the work of the Downtown Windsor Community Cooperative.)

Evangelicals have an ambivalent relationship to the broader culture. For many years we have extracted people from their neighborhoods and from the host culture and kept them busy with meetings and programs. Re-entering our neighborhoods and meeting people where they live feels strange and vulnerable. Yet "the word became flesh and dwelt among us." In Jesus God became weak and vulnerable. We are sent as Jesus was sent. We're not good at this; we tend to carry our baggage with us (cf. Luke 10).

In 2006 a Canadian seminary professor remarked to me that he could not identify a Canadian consensus around the meaning of community. I like Henri Nouwen's suggestion: the good news is that the Father invites us all to come home.[29] God is on a mission. Somewhere David Bosch remarked that, "It isn't the church of God that has a mission in the world, it's the God of Mission who has a Church in the world. In the current shift God is breaking down our definitions and resetting the boundaries."[30]

Frost and Hirsch share a story that captures the shift. A visitor to an Australian outback cattle ranch was intrigued by the seemingly endless miles of farming country with no sign of any fences. He asked a local rancher how he kept track of his cattle. The rancher replied, "Oh that's no problem. Out here we dig wells instead of building fences."[31]

Becoming missional has to do with where the boundary markers are being placed as we define the church. What is in-bounds? What is out-of-bounds? The boundary markers for the church should be determined by where the gifts and callings of God's people take them.[32] Or as one friend put it, "the work of the church is wherever God's people are situated." One of the prominent shifts in the way people connect in post-Christendom, where our faith stories are no longer shared currency, is by belonging before believing. Many of the stories collected in this volume reflect this open stance.

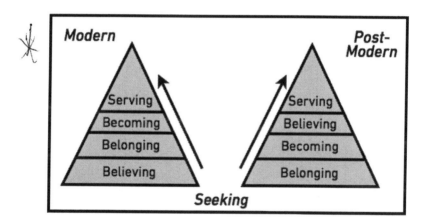

The traditional church makes it quite difficult for people to negotiate its maze of cultural, theological, and social barriers in order to get "in," and by the time newcomers have scaled the fences built around the church, they are so socialized as churchgoers that they are not likely to be able to maintain their connection with the social groupings they came from. So we lose contact with non-believers and we lose the ability to relate to them. We extract people from their natural habitats and substitute "attractional" and "come-to" structures for missional life.

If believers are to seize the opportunities God brings their way in the neighborhood and across society, and if they could proceed confident of support from others in the body, then "church" must be redefined. Instead of church as somewhere we go, church is where we live. Instead of extracting believers from their daily lives, we imagine them as missionaries in their communities, permeating society like salt and light.

If we organize ourselves around mission rather than around church, we will have to find new measures of success.[33] When we enter our neighborhoods in small and ordinary ways, we lose the drama of theater played out at carefully orchestrated meetings on Sunday mornings. Life becomes ordinary and simpler. When our dominant forms are more organic, we will find new ways to gauge growth. God was veiled in flesh in Jesus. The hiddenness of the incarnation, God at table with us, walking among us, calls us to a missional paradigm. Mission is our apostolic inheritance, a faithful response to God's grace in the places he roots us.

Mission Context and Church-Leavers

In Church After Christendom Stuart Murray reflects on what a missional movement will look like in post-modern culture.[34] He notes that we are now doing mission from the margins. Since we are no longer "at home," we must adjust our strategy, attitudes and expectations. What might this mean?

- It assumes less knowledge of Christianity
- It anticipates longer journeys to faith
- It allows others to set the agenda

But this latter point does not mean sitting back creating nice gatherings and hoping people will come. Rather, we must be infiltrating as well as inviting.

In chapter one David Fitch shows that in the old days of church planting twenty years ago (!) we didn't have to cross significant cultural barriers to make a convert. Mega-churches could be grown in large cities relatively quickly, because people knew the Christian stories. They might have attended Sunday school or Christian camp. Even if they had never crossed the threshold of a church, they may have been raised in Christian homes or heard the gospel on TV or radio. Increasingly this is not the case.

Mission Context

Church Members Core & Fringe

Open De-Churched

UnReached

Closed De-Churched

The group I am describing is the rapidly growing segment known as "Unreached." But in the meantime, a second segment is expanding rapidly: church-leavers, or the "de-churched." In *You Lost Me* Dave Kinnaman has broken church-leavers into three distinct groups, retaining some of the flavor of the research and conclusions of Alan Jamieson.

- Exiles
- Nomads
- Prodigals

Exiles and Nomads are on a spiritual journey, and the church doesn't seem to be answering their questions. We are mostly answering questions the last generation was asking, and the new questions sometimes make us uncomfortable.

Prodigals are those who doubt the truth of Christianity. Many have a degree of hostility toward the Church and have been hurt by Christians.

Exiles are particularly interesting. Many are ex-pastors and ex-leaders, revealing a disconnect between Church and faith. The dynamics of the institution often intrude and subvert their inward journey. Yet many retain a vital and evangelistic faith, and are strong followers of Jesus along with other Jesus followers who no longer fit into traditional church settings. Many exiles are artists and musicians.

Inward in Love

The Being of God

Outward in Mission

Exiles haven't walked away from faith in Christ, but have lost confidence in the institutional structures and programmatic trappings of the Church. For them these are distractions, a drain on time, resources, and energy that are better spent on mission. Skye Jethani breaks the de-churched down into two groups: the relationally de-churched ("The church is a machine; it doesn't know what to do with people"), and the missionally de-churched ("The church bids me 'come' when I think I'm actually supposed to be 'going' out on mission.")[35]

Ralph Winter uses the terms modality and sodality to talk about two different manifestations of the Church.[36] Modality points to structures of shared life, sodality points to mission. The two are like the phases of water: liquid and solid. Solid is more reliable, while liquid is more dynamic and flexible. But both are water, and both represent a truth about the Church.[37]

In these transitional times sodality is becoming more critical. Sodality may lack obvious structure and have a short life, like the rhizome. This thin and spidery web that supports this type of growth spreads underground and can exist for tens of yards without breaking the surface. It appears suddenly: you walk in the evening and you see only green grass. The next morning you spy three mushrooms, which exist for a day or two. and then disappear just as suddenly and mysteriously. The mushroom disappears, yet the hidden network remains, and may even be growing and expanding. The disappearance of the mushroom does not mean the network is unhealthy. Likewise, the short life of a "mushroom" church doesn't mean it was not significant in the economy of the Kingdom. Sometimes we attempt to preserve what we should let die. In an interview at *Next-Wave* Neil Cole comments,

The numbers of people can be deceptive. You can have many people and not be fruitful. You might just be putting on a better show than the guy around the corner. What we are looking for is fruitfulness.

For instance we don't care if our churches live a year, twenty years, or a hundred years. We care that while they live, they give birth. We may start a church that lasts a year, but while it lives, it births two daughter churches. That is a success. We think that if every church reproduces in that way, then the Kingdom of God will continue and grow.[38]

The Vision Trip

I was sitting with a brother who mentors church planters, both in Canada and in Europe. He was concerned that too many groups have continued to clone American models rather than allowing the new works to be shaped uniquely by the Holy Spirit. The first question church planting agencies often want to discuss is governance. Who is in control? How does leadership function? What structures are in place? Of course, when you are throwing denominational money at something accountability is important. But sometimes — and often, in the case of complex systems — centralized control is counter-productive. This is particularly true when centralized control is driven by corporate measures: attendance, buildings, cash.[39]

I recall Jesus' "wine and wineskin" analogy in Matthew and Luke. It seems that we want to give priority to the wineskin – perhaps familiarity gives us a sense of security. Sometimes perhaps we don't genuinely trust God or the people he anoints for the work, so we want control.[40] Maybe it gives us a sense of usefulness, or justifies our position, to maintain that level of input from a centralized office. Sometimes we would just rather have something concrete than have to trust in the Holy Spirit. Is that being too cynical, perhaps? David Fitch writes:

> There is a difference between a church gathered around a singular mission statement (even if written collegially by a group of leaders) and what I'd like to call a "shared imagination."

28

The first way to gather – via a mission/values/vision statement – is cognitive. It crafts words via a framework that has become so common in the business world. It then imposes this architecture onto the lives of its subjects.

The second way to gather – via a shared imagination – is holistic. It is the product of a shared process among a people who gather in a "place." Yes, we use words [but] we are discovering together what it means to commit our whole lives into what God is doing in this place ... [the posture] is one of mutual submission to the giftedness of the whole body including its more visible leaders.[41]

Apostolic teams are being recovered, and with them, missional imagination. We are in a transition zone where structures need greater flexibility, often seeming more liquid than solid. The language to describe these roles and their functioning varies, but the old command-and-control hierarchies are dying. J. R. Woodward identifies the new imagination for leadership as "polycentric."[42] Others, like Frost and Hirsch, talk about apostolic teams. The five-fold roles have familiar traits, with one exception. *In The Sky is Falling* Alan Roxburgh describes the poet as one who helps people make sense of their experiences.

John's prologue tells how Jesus "became flesh and lived among us." In a similar way, the poet shapes words so that what was hidden and invisible becomes known. Poets remove the veil and give language to what people are experiencing. This is only possible when the poet him/herself lives within the traditions and narratives of the people - "living reflexively in the traditions ... The poet listens to the rhythms and meanings occurring beneath the surface."

The leadership of poets, however, is not expressed in a modern manner. Poets "are not so much advice-givers as image and metaphor framers ... What churches need are not more entrepreneurial leaders with wonderful plans for their congregation's life, but poets with the imagination and gifting to cultivate environments within which people might again understand how their traditional narratives apply to them today ... Many of the programs on church health can only lead the churches down more of the same utilitarian and technological dead ends that have contributed to the current malaise."[43]

Inward/Outward – Adapted from Hirsch and Catchim, The Permanent Revolution

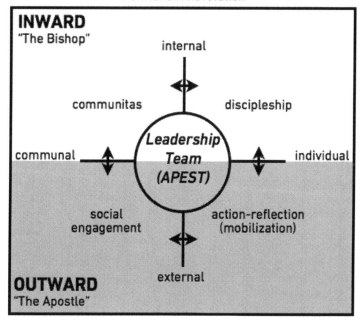

Finally, "poets make available a future that does not exist as yet; they are eschatologically oriented. From this environment, a missional imagination emerges."[44]

As we would expect, poets had little value in the churches of modernity. In modernity we sought to define problems toward a solution. But poets don't bring solutions; rather they bring questions that invite dialogue. Poets do not accept the view of a congregation as a tool for impacting the world, but as the location of God's work of redemption and the incipient present-future of the kingdom.

May God send us poets; may His Kingdom come!

Bibliography

Adams, Michael. *Fire and Ice: The United States, Canada, and the Myth of Converging Values.* Toronto: Penguin Canada, 2003.

Addison, Steve. *Movements That Change the World: Five Keys to Spreading the Gospel.* Grand Rapids: IVP, 2010.

Barna, George. *Revolution.* Carol Stream: Tyndale House, 2005.

Bass, Diana Butler. *Christianity for the Rest of Us:How the Neighborhood Church Is Transforming the Faith.* San Francisco: HarperCollins, 2006.

Bibby, Reginald W. *A New Day: Religion in Canadian Culture.* Lethbridge: Project Canada Books, 2012.

Brewin, Kester. *Signs of Emergence:A Vision for Church That Is Always Organic/Networked/Decentralized/Bottom-Up/Communal/Flexible/Always Evolving.* Grand Rapids: Baker, 2007.

Brueggemann, Walter. *Cadences of Home: Preaching Among Exiles.* Louisville: Westminster John-Knox, 1997.

Fitch, David E., and Geoff Holsclaw. *Prodigal Christianity: 10 Signposts into the Missional Frontier.* San Francisco: Jossey-Bass, 2013.

Fitch, David. "Mission Statement or Shared Imagination? How We Gather." *Reclaiming the Mission.* Online. No Pages: http://www.reclaimingthemission.com/?p=3290.

Friesen, Duane K. *Artists, Citizens and Philosophers: Seeking the Peace of the City.* Harrisonburg: Herald, 2000.

Frost, Michael, and Alan Hirsch. *The Shaping of Things to Come: Innovation and Mission for the 21st Century Church.* Peabody: Hendrickson, 2003.

Gibbs, Eddie. *LeadershipNext: Changing Leaders in a Changing Culture.* Downers Grove: IVP, 2005.

Gibbs, Eddie, and Ryan Bolger. *Emerging Churches: Creating Christian Community in Postmodern Cultures.* Grand Rapids: Baker Academic, 2005.

Goodmanson, Drew. "Triperspectival Ecclesiology." Online. No pages: http://www.goodmanson.com/leadership/triperspectival-leadership-diagram/.

Jethani, Skye. "Who are the De-Churched?" *Out of Ur.* Online. No pages: http://www.outofur.com/archives/2010/03/who_are_the_dec.html.

Kinnaman, Dave. *You Lost Me:Why Young Christians Are Leaving Church ... and Rethinking Faith.* Grand Rapids: Baker, 2011.

Homer-Dixon, Thomas. *The Upside of Down: Catastrophe, Creativity, and the Renewal of Civilization.* Toronto: Vintage Canada, 2007.

Klein, Naomi. *The Shock Doctrine: The Rise of Disaster Capitalism.* New York: Picador, 2007.

McNeal, Reggie. *The Present Future:Six Tough Questions for the Church.* San Francisco: Jossey-Bass, 2003.

Murray, Stuart. *Church After Christendom.* Waynesboro: Paternoster, 2004.

Myers, Joseph. *Organic Community: Creating a Place Where People Naturally Connect.* Grand Rapids: Baker, 2007.

Newbigin, Lesslie. *The Open Secret: An Introduction to the Theology of Mission.* Grand Rapids: Eerdmans, 1995.

Next-Wave. "Growing God's Kingdom from the Harvest: an Interview with Neil Cole by Next Wave. *CMA Resources.* Online No Pages: http://www.cmaresources.org/node/171.

Northcott, Michael. "From Environmental U-topianism to Parochial Ecology: Communities of Place and the Politics of Sustainability." *Ecotheology* 8 (2000) 71-85.

Nouwen, Henri. *Lifesigns: Intimacy, Fecundity, and Ecstasy in Christian Perspective.* New York: Doubleday, 1986.

Peterson, Eugene. *The Contemplative Pastor:Returning to the Art of Spiritual Direction.* Grand Rapids: William B. Eerdmans, 1989.

Petersen, Jim. *Church Without Walls: Moving Beyond Traditional Boundaries.* Colorado Springs: NavPress, 1992.

Ramachandra, Vinoth. *Subverting Global Myths: Theology and the Public Issues Shaping Our World.* Downers Grove: IVP Academic, 2008.

Roxburgh, Alan. *The Sky is Falling: Leaders Lost in Transition.* Eagle: ACI, 2005.

———. *Missional Map-Making: Skills for Leading in Times of Transition.* San Francisco: Jossey-Bass, 2010.

Sargent, Brad. "Ambles through Willow Creek's Reveal Part 3 Addendum-Assessing Ministry in Emerging Cultures." *Futuristguy.* Online. No pages: http://futuristguy.wordpress.com/2008/08/24/ambles-through-willow-creeks-reveal-part-3-addendum-assessing-ministry-in-emerging-cultures/#comment-684.

Sheldrake, Philip. *Spaces for the Sacred: Place, Memory, and Identity.* Baltimore: John Hopkins University Press, 2001.

Smith, James K.A. *Who's Afraid of Postmodernism?: Taking Derrida, Lyotard, and Foucault to Church.* Grand Rapids: Baker Academic, 2006.

The Archbishop's Council. *Mission-Shaped Church.* Trowbridge: The Cromwell Press, 2004.

Tickle, Phyllis. *The Great Emergence: How Christianity is Changing and Why.* Grand Rapids: Baker, 2008.

Tuan, YiFu. *Topophilia: A Study of Environmental Perception, Attitudes and Values.* Englewood Cliffs: Prentice-Hall, 1974.

Vanhoozer, Kevin J., et al. *Everyday Theology: How to Read Cultural Texts and Interpret Trends.* Grand Rapids: Baker Academic, 2007.

Wikimedia Foundation Inc. "Learning Community." *Wikipedia.* No pages. Online: http://en.wikipedia.org/wiki/Learning_community.

Winter, Ralph D. "The Two Structures of God's Redemptive Mission," Address to the All Asia Mission Consultation in Seoul, Korea, 1973.

Woodward, J.R. *Creating a Missional Culture:Equipping the Church for the Sake of the World.* Downers Grove: IVP, 2012.

---

1 Adams, *Fire and Ice.*

2 Bibby, "A New Day."

3 Barna, *Revolution.* See also the Pew Survey.

4 Kinnaman, *You Lost Me.*

5 Diana Butler Bass, Interview at http://blog.belief.net. July, 2009.

6 McNeal, *The Present Future.*

7 Brueggemann, *Cadences of Home.*

8 Homer-Dixon, *The Upside of Down*, 20-21.

9 Brewin in *Signs of Emergence* advocates the need for "liquid" structures rather than solid.

10 See in particular Eugene Peterson's take on problem solving. "Life is not so much a problem to be solved as a mystery to be explored." *The Contemplative Pastor*, 65.

11 I'm thinking in particular of Lesslie Newbigin's critique of the Church Growth movement in *The Open Secret.*

12 Murray, *Church After Christendom,* 113

13 Wikimedia Foundation Inc., "Learning Community."

14 Murray describes the key elements as story-telling, theological reflection, critical questioning, careful listening, passionate advocacy and thoughtful conclusion. *Church After Christendom,* 115.

15 Goodmanson, "Triperspectival Ecclesiology."

16 In their recent book *Prodigal Christianity* Fitch and Holsclaw describe the key characteristics of post-Christendom relative to mission as post-attractional, post-positional (authority) and post-universal.

17 Roxburgh offers such a diagram in his short book *The Sky is Falling*. See also Eddie Gibbs, "The Evolution of Hierarchy," in *LeadershipNext*. Egalitarian, participative models are more in congruence with the Trinity.

18 For example, Smith, *Who's Afraid of Postmodernism?*, Vanhoozer, *Everyday Theology*, Friesen, *Artists, Citizens and Philosophers*, Ramachandra, *Subverting Global Myths* and Roxburgh, *Missional Map-Making*. On the secular side, Homer-Dixon, *The Up Side of Down* and Klein, *The Shock Doctrine*.

19 For example, *Mission-Shaped Church* is a report from a working group within the Church of England and Gibbs and Bolger published *Emerging Churches*.

20 Most of our readers will also be familiar with Phyllis Tickle and her interesting take on the current shift, a "rummage sale" that occurs every five hundred years. *The Great Emergence*.

21 Ibid.

22 *The Present Future.*

23 See my coming book, *No Home Like Place.*

24 To join a network of friends exploring the gospel in place visit www.parishcollective.org.

25 On the importance of "place" as a concept in its own right, see Tuan, *Topophilia*.

26 Bass, *Christianity for the Rest of Us*, 38.

27 Peter Block writes, "The choice not to focus [on individual transformation] ... is because we have already learned that the transformation of large numbers of individuals does not result in transformed communities." Jeremiah 29:7 fits better as a mandate for the village church. More needs to be said regarding the built environment, and in particular, the city as place. See Sheldrake, *Spaces for the Sacred*, 147-171.

28 As a corrective to statist and globalizing framing of environmental policy. Northcott, "From Environmental Utopianism to Parochial Ecology," 71-85.

29 Nouwen, *Lifesigns.*

30 Source unknown.

31 Frost and Hirsch, *The Shaping of Things to Come.*

32 See Murray's discussion in *Church After Christendom,* 26, as well as Petersen, *Church Without Walls.*

33 An article by Brad Sargent, "Ambles through Willow Creek's Reveal Part 3 Addendum-Assessing Ministry in Emerging Cultures," offers not another assessment inventory, but an argument that using old tools results in zero validity. He writes that, "One of the major problems with applying existing assessment tools to situations in emerging cultures is that the tools' underlying cultural, theological, and philosophical presuppositions generally don't match with those of the cultures they claim to 'measure.' ... it's a test for apples being used on oranges ..."

34 *Church After Christendom,* 155

35 Jethani, "Who are the De-Churched?" Murray warns that Canadian Christians will soon be facing the challenge British Christians are already facing – developing mission strategies to engage with the burgeoning 'never-churched' rather than the diminishing constituency of the "de-churched." (Conversation with the author, 2010).

36 Winter, "The Two Structures of God's Redemptive Mission."

37 Brewin advocates the need for "liquid" structures rather than solid in *Signs of Emergence.*

38 Next-Wave, "Growing God's Kingdom from the Harvest."

39 See Addison, *Movements That Change the World* and also the writings of Roland Allen.

40 We are moving from "engineers," to "environmentalists." See Myers in *Organic Community.*

41 Fitch, "Mission Statement or Shared Imagination?"

42 Woodward, *Creating a Missional Culture.*

43 *The Sky is Falling*, 164-166.

44 Ibid., 166.

Jesus was going through all the cities and villages, teaching in their synagogues and proclaiming the gospel of the kingdom, and healing every kind of disease and every kind of sickness.

Seeing the people, He felt compassion for them, because they were distressed and dispirited like sheep without a shepherd. Then He said to His disciples, "The harvest is plentiful, but the workers are few. Therefore beseech the Lord of the harvest to send out workers into His harvest."

Matthew 9:35-38

Chapter 1

50 Years of Church Planting:
The Story as I See It
David Fitch

Over the last three decades, I have watched church planting change dramatically in Canada and the northern parts of the United States. Back in the 60s and 70s, we used to send fifteen or twenty people from one local church into another place several towns over that was "under-churched." We would hold worship services, teach Sunday School, have a children's ministry. We would set up shop. We would choose a pastor who "had all the tools" as they would say. He (most often a male) would be young, energetic and able to work like crazy. We would send out public announcements, expecting many who were looking for a church to just show up. And if we did the basic services well, then we assumed the little gathering would grow into a self-sustaining church in three years. In many ways, these church plants resembled franchises.

Church planting worked like this because there were still large numbers of Christians to draw from for a congregation. We were in the great post-World War II expansion in North America. New towns and subdivisions were springing up left and right. And just as each town needed a supermarket, a library and public schools, so also it needed a church. One could assume that out of the many thousands moving into these new habitats, some would be Christians in search of a new church home. So we planted churches like we would local grocery stores. This was the era of Christendom.

In the 80s, the focus on church planting changed. The post-World War II expansion had slowed. More and more suburban boomers had not returned to the churches of their youth. The focus of church planting shifted to recapturing these now-unchurched people for Christ. Now when we went to plant a church we needed to first conduct marketing surveys. We asked what we could do to make church more relevant and user-friendly.

The surveys focused on finding out what unchurched people were looking for. What about church turns them off? How can we do church in a way that relates to these people? How can we make church relevant so that they would come to our services? What could make church more attractive? We focused on delivering the services with "excellence" and "efficiency" characteristic of the marketplace. In these ways we planted churches like Wal-Marts. The seeker service and church growth methods were invented. Hundreds of boomer generation people came who had left the church a decade before. Many hundreds of people in traditional churches left as well for "the new and improved" big-box churches. Today, hundreds of mega-churches exist across North America as a testimony to the "success" of this approach to church planting.

Church planting like this worked because there were still huge numbers of unchurched people who had once learned of Christ in the earliest years of their upbringing. These unchurched had some familiarity with who Jesus was. Deep within their boomer psyches, Jesus still carried credibility, even authority, even if they did consider the church obsolete. We assumed therefore that if we could just make Jesus more relevant and attractive (as opposed to their former experiences of church) they would come.

If the Bible could be communicated in a way that was meaningful to people's everyday life and needs, these unchurched would surely listen. And they did come. People making "decisions for Christ" multiplied. Church planting like this, however, still depended upon what was left of the vestiges of North American Christendom. A majority of the conversions were former high-church catechumens "coming back to

Jesus."[1] They had never made a "personal" decision to follow the Jesus they had earlier been taught about (most often in catechetical rote fashion). In this way, the seeker church movement was built upon Christendom.

The days of Christendom are fading fast, causing a change in mindset of those who would plant churches. As the number of Christians without a church shrinks, and as the number of unchurched who once were catechumens of Christianity grows extinct, I have witnessed first-hand a new wave of church planters who think of church planting in completely different ways. They are not interested in competing for the leftovers of Christendom. They resist the notion that the church is in need of just one more innovation. They are interested in nothing less than becoming missionaries, to plant churches cross-culturally, to cross cultural barriers to people who have no knowledge or language about Jesus.

From Setting Up Grocery (Big-Box) Stores to Cultivating Gardens

For those of us born before 1970, this change is truly stunning. The landscape of post-Christendom demands we think about church planting with a new eye for faithfulness, truth and integrity. Among the new missional leaders, church is the name we give to a way of life, not a set of services. We do not plant an organized set of services; we inhabit a neighborhood as the living embodied presence of Christ. Missional leaders now root themselves in a piece of geography for the long term – becoming not only missional but also incarnational.

When we plant today, we survey the land for the poor and the desperate, not just in the physical sense but emotionally and spiritually as well. We seek to plant seeds of ministry, kernels of forgiveness, new plantings of the gospel among the poor (in every sense of the word) and then by the Spirit water and nurture them into the life of God in Christ. We gather on Sunday, but not for evangelistic reasons. We gather to be formed into a missional people and then sent out into the neighborhoods to minister grace, peace, love and the gospel of forgiveness and salvation.

The biggest part of church, then, is what goes on outside the Sunday gathering. If the old ways of planting a church were like setting up a grocery store, now it is more like seeding a garden, cultivating it, and watching God grow it amidst the challenges of the rocks, weeds and thorns. (I owe this metaphor to my co-pastors at Life on the Vine). What do these leaders look like? How can we walk alongside them? After hanging with a hundred or so of these leaders over the past few years, I have observed that missional leaders will most often be the following kinds of people.

Five Observations Concerning Missional Leaders

1. They Will Be Survivors

Enduring missional leaders must learn how to survive financially and spiritually for the long term. They must be able to hold down a job that does not consume them, but that enables them to live simply for the long term. In Christendom, the denominations used to pay someone to go plant a church. This would usually be one person who was unusually gifted and (based upon the above premises) could get a self-sufficient church going in three years. This person was in essence paid to extend an organization, open up a franchise, and set up a version of church that mirrored the distinctives of the denomination.

In the new post-Christendom, this doesn't make sense. In my opinion it takes at least five years of "seeding a community" before one even begins to see an ethos of community and new life develop that can be a cultural carrier-transmitter of the gospel. As a result, the new missional community leaders must have patience, steady faithfulness and the ability to live simply. They must be able to get jobs and not see the ministry as a privileged full-time vocation. They must have a mental image of how they are going to sustain their lives financially, relationally, spiritually and personally. This must take the shape of a sustainable rhythm. In my experience, these kinds of leaders are often found among the young and disenchanted evangelicals. I have learned they merely need a vision and a support network, and they are willing to sacrifice in ways my generation never would.

2. They Will be Communal Shepherds

I have found that missional leaders are most often shepherds of an overall ethos of a community. They are not starting and managing an organization. They may not even be good at organization. Instead they are cultivating a communal sense of mission identity among a gathering people "for this time and place." It used to be every church planter had to be an extrovert entrepreneur, someone who looked good and had the perfect family. Single people need not apply. This person had to be a good salesperson (man or woman) and had to have endless energy. He or she had to set a vision, direct a course, motivate and sell.

It's true that many of these qualities are helpful in starting new things. Yet I have seen, in this new era, that the missional leader is more often someone who can take time to be with people. He or she will listen to people, discern the needs, articulate where they are going, and knit the community together with gentleness, encouragement, and listening, in order to struggle as one. We do not gather as we once did to hear a charismatic leader preach an entertaining piece of inspiration. We do not gather for a professional piece of programmed worship experience. In the new post-Christendom we are coming together to be formed and shaped, supported and edified for the Mission as a band of brothers and sisters. Yes, we do gather on Sundays to hear the Word, to be nourished at the Table, and respond to what God is calling us to – but we do all this not as individuals but as a community, a community "sent out" on mission.

These kinds of leaders do not grow on trees; they must be mentored in character for the patience and faithfulness such shepherding requires. The Type-A person who is always selling or programming something has a role – don't get me wrong. But missional communities will not grow unless there is a nurturing, sustaining presence prodding and investing for the long term. Leaders who can adapt, roll with the punches, and shepherd communally are more valuable than the high-powered "strong starters" who wish to be on to the next thing in two years.

These new kinds of leaders are mentored not through leadership conferences and books, but in regular times together to practice together listening and mutual submission. They need to see love and consistency, and they need a guide, not a dictator.

3. They Will be Interpretive Leaders

Rarely do missional leaders lead their communities as the featured Bible teacher who dictates the Alpha and Beta of biblical doctrine. Rather they are interpreters of what God is doing communally through the teaching and preaching of Scripture. They read Scripture in community and preach looking for what God is calling them to in the neighborhood. It used to be that every church planter was a gifted preacher who could draw the crowds. Those days are past.

They are past, not because you cannot attract dissatisfied or thrill-seeking Christians from other churches with a great preacher, but because we have seen that true spiritual growth occurs communally only when the whole congregation is involved in times of praying, hearing, submitting and responding to the Word. Interpretive leaders[2] do not dictate from the pulpit a list of do's and don'ts and solutions from God for every problem. They interpret the Scriptures to open our eyes to what God is doing and where He is taking us. In other words, they cultivate other interpreters and listeners.

In a different way then, we must mentor leaders who are more than great preachers. They must lead their communities in seeing what God is doing via the lens of Scripture. "Where is God taking us, where is he calling us?" How do we respond faithfully in this time and place?

The sermons and teaching of missional leaders, therefore, fuel the corporate imagination of God's Kingdom in our midst and where He is at work in our everyday lives. And when conflicts arise, we sit and pray; we submit to one another, and pray for courage and humility; and we study the Scriptures in order to discern the journey we are being called to make in God's mission. This kind of leader often does not come from our (all too often) modernist seminaries. They are grown in a community which gathers to worship the Triune God so as to discern him at work in our midst.

4. They Will be Directors of Spiritual Formation

I believe that missional leaders must know how to guide the community in spiritual formation. Admittedly, this kind of leadership is not common, at least among younger evangelicals. Yet I still believe that the development of communal worship liturgies that are historically thick yet still local and organic is crucial for these times. We now recognize that the consumerist forces of our post-Christendom Canada (and even worse in the United States) cannot be resisted as isolated individuals. An individual alone cannot resist the forces of desire that tell us a five-bedroom house, and two new cars are more important than Mission, the very life we share with the Triune God. Our communities therefore must be places of spiritual formation, of resistance to the forces of distraction, unsatiated desire and exploitation of those we choose not to know.

This means that our Sunday/Saturday gatherings must be places of spiritual formation, encouragement and sending out for Mission. We must ever navigate against putting on a show that will attract; rather we must develop a liturgy that is simple, accessible and Scriptural, and that guides our lives into Christ and guards us from the distractions that would take us away from Mission. I know that liturgy is a difficult pill these days for the newly arriving missional leaders to swallow. But there will be no missional community of people formed and shaped for mission if we just preach Mission as a legalistic requirement. Mission requires patience, a sense of vision, and a level of self-denial that can only be formed inwardly in living bodies, trained in the simple organic disciplines and liturgies of the historic Church.

5. They Will be Leaders who Give Away Power

Missional leaders who have served for any length of time have learned how to die to their egos and allow God to use every man's and woman's gifts in the community for the furtherance of his Kingdom. Hierarchy is the product of Christendom.[3] It harks back to a day when Christianity still held power in society, when Jesus was still established as a given in Canada. (Even when the Jesus of liberal Protestantism dominated Canada, there still remained a basis for authority and a respect for who Jesus was.)

Hierarchy made sense in a day when the preacher in the town was looked up to and held power. This old world, when one man could wield influence and get things done in the name of Christ, is waning. As a result, no one man or woman can lead a community from the top down and expect the church to go on as a viable social reality. We cannot be the very Body of Christ if we do not empower the manifold gifts in the community to minister the Kingdom as part of everyday life. If we even try to operate out of the old hierarchical ways, missional communities will flounder and their leaders will die from exhaustion. I have seen it happen over and over.

It is my belief therefore that missional leadership needs always to be multiple. Most missional pastors/leaders need to be bi-vocational (bi-ministerial) for their own survival. Such leaders must learn to mutually submit to the other leaders as they guide the journey of the community. They must mutually learn to mentor leaders and give away power. Different strengths should be recognized among leaders and then multiply that leadership (following the APEST model of Frost and Hirsch's The Shaping of Things to Come).

This model subverts the CEO pastorate style we have all become so used to because each pastor gives away power instead of consolidating it. This kind of pastoral leadership models a living body for the rest of the community to see, instead of dictating to the rest of the church to "just do it." In this way, all shall own the leadership of this community and the journey we are on in the Mission. This kind of leadership needs to be mentored, modeled and practiced, and it never comes easy.

	Functional 20th Century Church Technical Skills	Emerging Missional Church Adaptive Skills
Environmental	• Stable • Predictable • Developmental	• Unstable • Discontinuous • Emergent
Organizational Culture	• Hierarchies • Bureaucracies • Managers/Experts • Top-Down Flow • Strategic Planning • Linear • Fragmentation	• Networks/Teams • Dialogue/Conscious Learning • Cultivated Diversity • De-Centered • Converging Conversations • Bottom-Up • Non-Linear • Integration
Leadership Functions	• Manage People • Optimize Performance • Control Structure	• Empower People • Nurture Teams • Invite Participation • Cultivate Environments

Adapted from Roxburgh, *The Sky is Falling.*

Missional Leaders and the Promise of Missional Orders

All of the above paints a picture of not just a new kind of leader, but also a new vision of what the Canadian church can look like in post-Christendom. There is an invigorated ecclesiology emerging here among these up-and-coming church planters. This view of church places an emphasis on forming a social life together that is rich in community. Inherent in this social life is the drive to be hospitable, open communities that invite the stranger into our midst, telling Our Story, ministering the grace and healing of the gospel. We will take up space, not as a defensive enclave, but as the manifestation of his reign ahead of time for all to see and experience.

This view of church says we must dedicate ourselves to a specific geographic area for many years at a time. We must inhabit this geography for Christ and discern where God is at work in those who cross our paths daily. We must look for the hurting and confused across this landscape, every day seeking to incarnate Christ to them. And we must patiently listen to our neighbors, blessing them and praying for their restoration.

This long-term presence in our neighborhoods makes mission to the lost within post-Christendom possible. This new sense of ecclesia knows we must live all of the above as a way of life born out of our relationship with the Triune God revealed in our Lord Jesus Christ. We must engage together in rhythmic transformational practices of spiritual formation that order our lives into God. Only in this way can we avoid becoming a new kind of social justice legalistic "holiness." Many will recognize in this description some of the Rule of St. Benedict including the rule of *conversatio* (community), *hospitalitas* (hospitality), *stabilitas* (geography), and *obedientia* (transformative practices of mutual submission). This is the way of missional orders – an expression of Kingdom life that can root missional communities in the new post-Christendom of the West.

Birthed out of this view of Christ's Church, emerging missional leaders imbibe a mentality that is drastically different from the church planter of the past. They lead in ways more akin to an Abbot (or Abbess) of a medieval missional order than an entrepreneurial wiz-kid of the typical franchise start-up church. They possess character like a patient gardener as opposed to the restless CEO numbers-cruncher. Indeed, most (not all) of the missional leaders I have met already exemplify strains of the new mentality. I believe this bodes well for the future. For I believe this new generation of pastors provides hope for a renewal of Christianity in Canada. They are already leading communities, house churches and monastic-like orders all over the country.

Like a fermenting revolution evolving out of a tired and reified ancien regime, these tiny bands of Christians have come on the scene committed to live a shared life of worship, spiritual formation, community, hospitality, and service to the poor (of all kinds). In ways never imagined by the machinations of the evangelical mega-church, many of these bands are already infecting their neighborhoods with an embodied gospel that cannot be denied – only responded to.

Knowing Christendom is gone, these new leaders carry no pretensions. Instead they embody the gospel in its most compelling, authentic, non-coercive form. This new wave of Christians is small in number and possesses little to no resources financially. Most do not impress with their grandiose visions. They do not hang out in the halls of power. They do not make a show of their successes. Yet their vision of a simple Christian habitat as witness to the world reminds me of the Irish missional orders God used to effect a profound conversion of European society in the fourth century. We have seen the world changed like this once before (read How the Irish Saved Civilization by Thomas Cahill). Could we be in the early stages of seeing God move in a similar fashion once again? Let us pray it be so.

About David Fitch

David Fitch is the founding pastor of Life on the Vine Christian Community--an emerging/missional church affiliated with the Christian and Missionary Alliance in the northwest suburbs of Chicago (www.lifeonthevine.org). David is also Lindner Professor of Evangelical Theology at Northern Seminary in Lombard, Illinois. He is the author of *The Great Giveaway* and co-author, with Geoff Holsclaw, of *Prodigal Christianity*.

Bibliography

Carroll, Colleen. *The New Faithful: Why Young Adults Are Embracing Christian Orthodoxy*. Chicago: Loyola, 2002.

Fitch, David E., and Geoff Holsclaw. *Prodigal Christianity: 10 Signposts into the Missional Frontier*. San Francisco: Jossey-Bass, 2013.

---

1 Ironically many denominations still categorize these "decisions" as "conversion growth." Meanwhile more and more youth are leaving evangelical low churches for the high church traditions. (See Carroll, *The New Faithful*). I wonder if the high church traditions count them as (re)conversions as the low church evangelicals once did when their youth converted to evangelicalism?

2 I owe this term to my friend Jim VanYperen.

3 For an expanded discussion of this key characteristic of post-Christendom, see Fitch and Holsclaw, *Prodigal Christianity*.

50

God is beyond in the midst of our life.
The church stands,
not at the boundaries where human powers give out,
But in the middle of the village.

Dietrich Bonhoeffer

Chapter 2

Awaken's Story, Calgary
Scott Cripps

Awaken is a question-formed community. We asked honest questions and we are seeking honest answers. Often we can ask questions where we already assume we know the answers. Or we can ask questions, but our minds are made up. For Awaken, as it was for Neo in the over-quoted and over-metaphored movie, *The Matrix* – "It's the question(s) that drives us." Certainty is a tempting mistress and without questions we often fall back to the place where we feel the most secure, the place where we are the most familiar. So it is with much humility that I contribute to this book, for Awaken has not arrived yet... in fact we are still very much in the process of discerning, listening and asking. This chapter will provide a snapshot of Awaken, a small community of believers in the northwest corner of Calgary who are striving to be faithful to the calling God has placed on us.

Awaken has been a work of God. There is no other way to understand it; in fact, there is no other way we should ever understand the Church. As much as technique, personality and charisma can attract a crowd to form a community, the church's roots, foundation and ongoing work on earth are based in the very heart of God who desires his people to gather, demonstrate and proclaim his transformative power. This heartbeat of Jesus is what Awaken is trying to encompass.

Awaken began as the third service of a contemporary Canadian Baptists of Western Canada church in northwest Calgary. It was originally designed to attract and reach postmodern folks who weren't likely to darken the doorway of a traditional Sunday morning church service. In order to accomplish this, it went down the pathway of "experiential worship" where each Sunday there needed to be some sort of element of participation, or creative expression, or just things done differently.

It was into this situation that I entered the equation. I was serving as the youth pastor at this church and eventually my role grew to include Awaken, and God drew together a community where we could learn and journey together. It wasn't long into this experience that I realized that living under the umbrella of an established church wasn't allowing us to risk, venture, and really grow into what God was calling us to be. I felt initially that Awaken was simply "playing church" and had yet to take steps towards really understanding what it meant to be the Church. It was at this point that we began to ask questions such as: "What is the gospel?" "What is the Church?" "What is the Kingdom?" and "What does justice look like?" It was also at this point that we began to dream, pray, and discern where the missio Dei was going to lead us.

I never really saw myself as a church planter; in fact while going to university, I didn't really envision myself as a pastor. I stumbled into the ministry through the backdoor as staffing changes had caused an opening within the youth ministry, and I was hired to run the programs as a part-time job while I finished my degree in political science from the University of Calgary.

But God had other ideas. He kept bringing mentors, authors, teachers and friends into my life, and the result was a community formed and launched into the neighborhood of Bowness. Awaken is a community that is willing to turn from a comfortable existence in a larger church, to being homeless and relying on the hospitality of others. We are a community that is willing to embrace the unknown together and to keep asking questions.

A New Imagination

My journey of leading and participating with Awaken down this pathway to a missional existence in a new neighborhood is the result of a number of factors. New imagination is needed to venture out into the unknown and for myself this new imagination came together (and is coming together) by seeking and listening to voices among and beyond ourselves. It is easy to live within the comforts of your own reality; it is a greater challenge to be open to moving beyond the limits of your experience.

There are two major factors that provided impetus to Awaken taking steps to becoming a missional community.

First of all, God brought together a willing and passionate group of people. Community has been a key for us. Personally my wife (Leanne) and daughters (Hannah, Ella, and Lily) felt God calling us to live a simple life among folks who are different from us in a neighborhood that had a diverse reality to it. But we gained courage and resolve when this vision was shared beyond ourselves into our community and others were willing to venture out with us. It is through these relationships we have with each other that we've been able to become something we are not by ourselves.

One story of Awaken's resolve and blessing was to release my family and me on a seven-month leave of absence right at the point where we had decided to commit to being a church plant. A number of folks who heard that I was going to be stepping away asked who was going to replace me and preach while I was gone. They were asking that question rooted in an ecclesiology where only a trained clergy could lead, preach and guide a community. Fortunately Awaken had long since grown beyond that imaginative limit, and not only remained afloat but actually deepened the sense of community and commitment to our vision.

This experience of stepping away resulted in us all learning a number of lessons that we couldn't have learned if my family and I did not relinquish the role of being the sole owner of the vision. We learned that the Spirit of God does reside in his people, and in doing so gifts and equips everyday folks to contribute and lead in cultivating an expression of God's church. We learned that who we are and what abilities and resources we have are not merely adequate but are powerful enough to demonstrate God's transformative power. We learned that leadership is not one person who knows all and does all, but rather occurs as a relational process among people. And finally we learned that through the ups and downs, the challenges and victories, God is good.

The second major factor in Awaken's story was that God began to bring people into my life who helped me to see a bigger picture. The first was my theology professor, Mabiala Kenzo. Kenzo was the first person who put the book, Missonal Church, into my hands. It was under his teaching that I saw a much bigger picture of the Church in God's plan. I took every theology course I could at Canadian Theological Seminary including a course in Narrative Theology that added depth to my understanding of Scripture. As a Christian I first acknowledged Jesus when I was a child, but with Kenzo, a second conversion occurred: a love for the Church and for God's mission through the Church into the world. I realized that despite people's sentiments, you cannot love Jesus and hate the Church. They can't be separated. It was with this ecclesial foundation that I became passionate about cultivating a community where we could pursue the vision together.

The second person God brought into my life was Cam Roxburgh. Cam is the pastor of Southside Community Church in BC's Lower Mainland and the head of Church Planting Canada. It was at a church planting conference in Toronto in 2005 that Cam and I met, and it was there that Cam extended an invitation to my family to come out to Vancouver and to see and experience Southside firsthand.

Awaken gave us with their blessing and in December 2006 we arrived in Vancouver. During my time at Southside I was able to join a community that had incarnated the gospel into five different neighborhoods, and I was able to witness the character and competencies of the leaders who were leading Southside into these neighborhoods. I saw the power of a covenant that held everyone together and focused folks on the task that God had called them to. I saw the amazing ability of everyday folk to be mentored into leadership, and then lead communities into their missional existence. And I saw the heart of missional leaders and their love for God, each other and their neighborhoods.

The third person God had brought across my path was someone who has known me forever: my uncle Bob Swann. Uncle Bob and Aunt

Anne have always been heroes to me. They have spent the majority of their adult lives living out the mission of God to folks in Kenya and Somalia, as well as to refugees in Toronto and homeless folks on Vancouver's Downtown Eastside. When we ventured out to Vancouver to connect with Southside, it was my Uncle Bob and Aunt Anne who opened their home to my family and welcomed us in. Living with them we were exposed to people whose heart beat for the marginalized, the poor, the refugees, and the sick. I was exposed to an aspect of the gospel that I had neither explored nor seen up close.

While living with Uncle Bob, my family and I were surrounded by stories of God's Kingdom breaking into the midst of folks who were living in the toughest of circumstances. We were invited to experience that reality by accompanying my uncle on a number of occasions through the streets of Vancouver and to the shelter he ran through First Baptist Church.

Through these three voices, theology, neighborhood, and justice began to become the primary ingredients in what God was serving up with Awaken. Each of these lenses allowed me to see beyond the limits of my own vision, and to catch a glimpse of a more holistic gospel, shaping a richer ecclesiology.

Where the Streets are Not Marked

In September 2007, Awaken began to gather on Sunday evenings in the neighborhood of Bowness in northwest Calgary. Unlike most of Calgary, Bowness is a very old and established neighborhood. It once existed as its own town prior to being engulfed as part of Calgary in the 1960s. It is not a monochromatic community where everyone looks the same, talks the same, buys the same, and consumes the same; on the contrary, it is eclectic and diverse.

Bowness exists as an independent piece of geography in Calgary with the Trans-Canada highway, the Bow River and two bridges at either end providing clear territorial markers. For most Calgarians there are no reasons to drive through Bowness: it is not a shortcut to some destination, nor is it a neighborhood with much to draw or attract people (except for Bowness Park). Yet Bowness has a strong sense of identity. The majority of the folks in this 10,000-person neighborhood consider themselves Bownesians and proudly display "I ♥ Bowness" bumper stickers or t-shirts. In Calgary, Bowness has a reputation of being a troubled neighborhood, a descriptor not completely without warrant since it has the fourth highest murder-rate in the city.

Awaken's desire is to weave itself into the fabric of this neighborhood and to engage the social justice issues while also inviting others to become followers of Jesus. To accomplish this, a number of strategic elements form us. First, in order to missionally engage a neighborhood, the people must be valued as neighbors, not projects. This is especially true in Bowness where there is such a strong, independent identity. You cannot be an outsider; you must be part of the community, and you must wear the mantle of Bowness with pride.

My family and I purchased a half-duplex where we rent out the basement and the five of us live on the top floor sharing 950 square feet, two bedrooms and one bathroom. It's cozy but it also represents what we want to be about: a simple family that relies on relationships to define us rather than stuff. After six months into this journey, two other members of Awaken purchased property in Bowness, and most of the others are looking to do the same when they are able to enter the market. Our own experience of living in the neighborhood means that my oldest daughter can walk to school, we can meet and love the other kids, families and people around us, and we can pray and gain a sense of what God is up to in this place.

Church planting in a post-Christendom context also means that one of your strategies must be to forego past methods and measures of success. It cannot be about attendance, owning a building and having a six- or seven-figure budget. Therefore we recognize that the margins are the place to call home. Instead of trying the find the best piece of real estate and attracting people through the widest array of programs, smallness and vulnerability are an opportunity. We are the ones without a home, without power, and without a clue, and so God can use us.

The vulnerability of the early disciples is seen in Luke 10, where Jesus sends them with nothing, to go as innocent as lambs, and to rely on the hospitality of strangers. Awaken has been blessed to accept this role and the reality of God going before us. And in doing so, Awaken now has partners, such as Bow Waters Community Church, who have provided us with their small facility to gather on Sunday evenings, and a plot of land to start a community garden. The Bowness Community

Association invited me to be on their board to help re-establish its presence in the neighborhood. Awaken has realized that instead of trying to carve out and claim our piece of the turf, we will best reach people through the relationships we build in common ways as we seek to enhance the well-being of our neighbourhood.

Another reality of church planting in a post-Christendom era is that it requires creative approaches to ensure longevity and the commitment to the neighborhood. I believe that becoming bi-vocational is a key strategic reality for church planters. Adopting a bi-vocational model has allowed Awaken to dream of means of blessing the neighborhood (a "third space" and community garden) instead of focusing all of its finances on one salary. Moreover, we have maintained the ethos of Awaken to go forward by relying on everyone to help create our expression of the church. There is no full-time pastor who is paid to do everything, know everything, and be everything.

My transition into bi-vocationality has gone quite smoothly. I am fortunate to be connected to an online software company that believes in what we are doing. This company has hired me to provide client support and data management on a three-quarter-time basis. It recognizes that I will occasionally need to have lunch or coffee with folks. This has been nothing short of a Godsend, and I can't help but wonder if more Christian business folks began to view their enterprises as means of supporting missional endeavors and church planting, what a difference that could make. This job along with a part-time salary from Awaken allows me to stay in the neighborhood, support my family, pay our bills, and stay committed to Bowness regardless of how Awaken's finances may fluctuate.

"On You Will Go"

Having arrived in Bowness and having begun to establish relationships and make inroads into the fabric of the neighborhood, a new question has arisen in our midst: How do you stay faithful to the calling and mission God has placed upon you? This is a vital question and a question of spiritual formation. We have come to the conclusion that submitting ourselves to a covenant or rule would allow us to all share a common vision, a common mission, and common practices to ensure our faithfulness to the calling. This is our covenant in its most recent form. We call it our SENT Covenant:

S - Story
We affirm the historic and orthodox Christian faith. We believe that God has revealed himself through the Holy and Inspired Scriptures. We believe that God has invited us to be rooted in him and his desires to bring wholeness and peace towards others, towards the earth, towards himself, and within ourselves.

Covenant: We covenant to root ourselves in the biblical narrative.

E - Eat
We affirm the necessity of practices that provide us with the eyes to see and the ears to hear God in the everyday moments of our lives. We believe in engaging in spiritual disciplines that allow us to see, listen, taste and touch the reality of God and that prompt us to remain faithful to the path God has called us to.

Covenant: We covenant to engage in spiritual practices that keep us focused on our journey to be conformed to the image of Jesus. (eat, pray, tithe, solitude, art, writing, exercise...)

N - Neighborhood
We affirm our role, as God's people, to serve and bless others. The Church as the body of Jesus is to follow His example and share his heart for others in our broken and fragmented world. We believe in following Jesus towards those who are suffering and facing injustice and living out the redemptive and transformative message of hope that is found in Jesus.

Covenant: We covenant to love and serve others in our neighborhoods.

T - Together
We affirm that everyone bears God's image. Through sharing in each other's sufferings and celebrations, loving and forgiving one another, we can journey forward. We were made for community and within loving relationships, God's truth takes on flesh and blood, and we are not alone. We believe that together through Jesus we can become more than we are individually.

Covenant: We covenant to pursue God together in community

Another aspect of spiritual formation for Awaken is observing the Christian calendar. Our Sunday gatherings are opportunities for us to eat, worship, share, receive teaching, and focus ourselves around the major moments in Jesus' life. To do this, Awaken has created a calendar that guides us on eight journeys each year. Each journey is led by a team of people at Awaken and involves cultivating an environment where we can learn and experience together the theme or movement of that particular journey. (See illustration A below).

Finally, a vital piece to our spiritual formation and our mission in Bowness is our small groups. Awaken currently has five small groups that gather together throughout the week. The groups are small (four to seven people each), and exist to provide a sense of community and a sense of mission together. The small groups corporately hold to the SENT covenant, and as a result the small groups can discern which practices will best suit them, and what aspects of justice, compassion, environmental stewardship, or service they can provide to Bowness. We are just in the process of launching these small groups and for many of us, it is the first time we will have submitted to a covenant or rule that binds us all together. We are praying that instead of being viewed as restricting and limiting, we will see that the covenant provides the center from which we can all launch and pursue God as he brings wholeness to ourselves, our neighbors, and the earth.

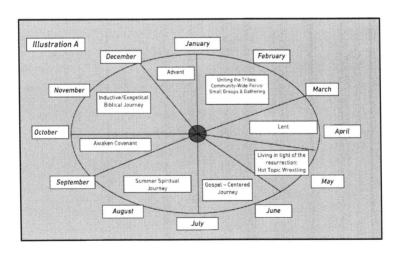

"Your Mountain is Waiting"

I think I've shared enough of our vision, so let me end with a story. When I was a child, Christmas morning was a big deal. I lived in a home that was fortunate enough to have Santa Claus come visit every year and bring awesome gifts and presents. In the year leading up to my tenth Christmas, I was anxiously looking forward to a new remote-controlled car that I had been asking for. I lived in a cul-de-sac that didn't have much traffic, and I could already imagine how I would steer the car around different obstacles and materials that lay outside my front door.

Christmas Eve arrived, and I couldn't sleep, or at least I didn't sleep for long. Sometime in the middle of the night I awoke with excitement and anticipation. The house was dark and quiet, yet I was awake and alert. I quietly crept down the stairs to see if my wishes had come true. And there before my eyes were three stockings and three piles of gifts laid out, one for my sister, my brother, and myself.

The first thing I noticed was this large remote-controlled monster truck and I went right for it. I picked up the large box and began to drool over the possibilities of having a monster truck instead of just a car. Yet as I begin to look through the stocking and the other gifts in that pile, I saw that this was not for me, but rather this was my little brother's gift from Santa. So I quickly turned to the other stocking and pile of gifts and I saw another remote-controlled vehicle. This time it was a van ...

A van ... In my pile from Santa was a little remote-controlled van. What was Santa thinking?! How could my five-year-old brother get the monster truck, and I get the small van? So I looked around and made the switch. I reasoned that Santa surely must have made a mistake, and that since I was the older brother, I clearly should be the one with the larger remote-controlled vehicle, and surely not a van!

I snuck back into my room, closed the door. I tried to go back to sleep but I couldn't. Eventually the sun began to rise and I ventured out of my room. I had done some thinking and realized that there is no way Santa could make a mistake. Either my brother behaved like an angel and deserved the monster truck, or I had been a brat and was punished with the van: either way I decided to accept the reality and I hustled down the stairs to switch back the gifts. I had just made the switch back when the rest of the family entered the room. There were smiles and cries of excitement from everyone, especially from my brother when he saw his truck. I pretended like I was surprised and pleased with what Santa had brought me, but all the time I was watching my brother and his truck and had gently set my van down, still in its box, to the side.

My father noticed this and came over. He grabbed the van and sat down with me to open it. He noticed the way I was watching my brother and the monster truck and told me to watch closely. As I watched, I noticed something about the monster truck: it was large, but it was meant for a little child. The control was not remote, but was attached permanently to the truck. It couldn't go fast or do any cool tricks. All you could do was walk behind and steer it as in crawled along in a small, simple way. Meanwhile my Dad had taken the van out of its packaging, and I realized that this was the true remote-controlled vehicle. Although I was not envisioning a van, it more than accomplished what I hoped the remote-controlled vehicle would. It would race around our cul-de-sac and through the courses I had set up at incredible speeds. It was the vehicle I was meant to have and I realized that Santa had got it right all along.

Awaken's story is our story. It is the dream my family and I and our amazing little community is meant to live out. God has always got it right; we just have to not be afraid and believe. We traded in the large monster truck for our little remote-controlled van when we walked out of the large established church and moved into Bowness.

Now as a fluid little group, empowered by the Holy Spirit and moved by the heartbeat of our Savior, we finally get to run through the course designed for us. It is the path least taken, but it is one we walk together. There are still plenty of obstacles. We are still trying to figure out what leadership looks like. Friends we thought would continue with us have stepped away. And we are still learning to love. But we are free to go where the wind blows us, dream dreams that we never thought were possible, and keep asking questions to prompt us to faithfulness. Soon a community garden will exist in Bowness, and a coffee shop or a "third space" will be coming. Lord willing, struggling folks will find us and will experience the grace and mercy of our Lord Jesus. To him be the Glory.

About Scott Cripps

Scott Cripps loves venturing out into the great unknown and being a part of new things. Currently this involves Awaken and FAME (www.fameassets.com), a new, cutting-edge company. He is married to Leanne, who fosters an organic, environmental, alternative existence for Scott and their three girls.

Chapter 3

BREATHE, Richmond
Phil Harbridge

BREATHE Christian Society formed and began "breathing" in October 2004 as an independent and informal family meeting in the author's home in Richmond, British Columbia. It was a simple and rudimentary beginning to a spiritual community. BREATHE was not a church plant, nor a denominationally-financed outpost. Instead it was a gathering of family and friends with no budget, an ambiguous vision, and yet the certainty that we were doing the right thing in the right place.

In recent decades the church has learned again to deal in experiences – to focus on weaving together the daily experiences of life with an everyday faith. Faith communities are committed to offering spiritual fragments to those who are on a quest and rethinking their beliefs. As these people begin constructing a theology of their own, fragments of the Christian narrative are often used. As Steve Taylor indicates, "Many people today are spiritual tourists—willing to stroll the pick-and-mix supermarket of spiritual options, looking for spiritual practices. They search out ritual and mystery, hoping for relevance and cultural coherence. They want an individualism holistically connected with others."[1]

Spirituality is "in the air" (just Google "spirituality" and read any of the 80 million hits.) For centuries God's people have toured or made journeys: from Abraham's sojourn into Canaan to Israel's wilderness wanderings, from the Via Dolorosa to Paul's missionary journeys, from medieval pilgrimages to the literary imagery of John Bunyan's writings. But as each of these examples proves, the journey is rarely linear. Our journey is to encounter the living God, the God who really exists. The question is: What will take us there? What will help us on that journey?

My wife and I and our two daughters have lived in Richmond since 1992, and in our current home in the Seafair area of Richmond since 1999. The City of Richmond website describes the city as:

> ... a culturally diverse and geographically unique community centrally located on Canada's west coast, in Greater Vancouver, 20 minutes from downtown Vancouver, and 25 minutes from the US border. With a population of over 181,942 people, Richmond is a growing dynamic urban centre with a unique mix of residential, and commercial property, agricultural lands, industrial parks, waterways and natural areas ... Much of the recent population growth has been made up of Asian immigrants. People of Chinese or South Asian ancestry now represent nearly sixty percent of Richmond residents.[2]

Fortunately, many people in the greater Vancouver area (Vancouver, Richmond, Surrey, White Rock, New Westminster, Burnaby) easily move between cities for work, worship, and recreation. This means that any church or faith community can be considered accessible regardless of one's suburb of residence. According to the Yellow Pages, there are currently 69 religious groups or churches in Richmond that meet on a regular basis.

After transitioning out of a rewarding and complex ministry in a large traditional urban church, our family felt unmotivated to re-enter another traditional church community. Trading one church for another was not at the top of our list of priorities; however, encountering God in a fresh and mysterious way, was. Fortunately, after resigning from our previous church and moving past some of the bittersweet events of the final weeks, our daughters had not become jaded in their faith or distanced themselves from shared worship experiences. God was very much alive, craved our worship, and not only loved us but was very fond of us. Many years had been invested with families and young people in our former church, and God had blessed us with rich relationships and fruitful ministry. Although our spirits were buoyant toward God, we also felt needy as a family. We had become weary of regularly giving, serving, and supporting others in their spiritual maturation sometimes at the expense of our own. The political landscape in our previous church and the routine of predictable worship had taken its toll. We believed that there was so much more, so much deeper life, and richer worship experiences that God had in store for us. Our family was primed and craving a breath of fresh air from God.

Instead of frantically readying ourselves to venture out in search of a church building, we felt compelled to simply show up in our own living room and invite God to meet with us. We did not want to be distracted with style, or fashion, or appearances, or image, or carpet or anything else that has so often marred the focus of churchgoers. Our first gatherings in the fall of 2004 were marked by simplicity, intimacy, and honesty. We were a family, and we were worshipping. We sought to weave together what we believed with how we behaved, to worship and experience God in real life, in a place where we most often live life. As creatively as possible we sought to encounter God and experience his character. Group and personal readings, lighting candles of presence, singing and listening to music, silence, a delicious brunch, and lively dialogue all filled our first breaths. For several weeks this continued. No two weeks were ever the same, though every week God's Spirit led us into a deeper communion with, and appreciation of, Jesus. Occasionally the dogs would interrupt us or we'd laugh at the meandering conversation, but it felt natural, and it made sense to be at home, with God.

A few friends who had heard that we were setting aside time on Sunday mornings to focus on God started to join in on the humble gatherings. As a family we had not looked to assemble as many worshippers as we could. God seemed to be showing up in our small worship gatherings, and that was deeply satisfying and enriching. Honest, authentic God-seekers, however, slowly became curious, then interested, and eventually committed to setting aside time each week to be together with God.

For several weeks this nondescript, fragile, needy community drew together around God without any thought of ecclesiological structure. Some people explored the group for a time and moved on, while others found a home. It was suggested by one of the participants that perhaps we try to organize ourselves without compromising the spontaneity and flexibility of our worship. Given the size of the group and our affirmation of shared leadership, structure seemed irrelevant except for the value of accountability, decision-making, growing awareness, and potentially charitable status.

In January 2005, after agreeing that the name BREATHE characterized the desire of our community to fill our lungs and life with God, a skilled young lawyer from the group filled out the government applications to formally organize and register our community as a church. By February 2005, BREATHE Christian Society was formed as an incorporated Society in the province of British Columbia, and two months later became a federal charitable organization.

From first breath to formally recognized church community, the focus has never strayed from breathing in God's Spirit and life, encountering the Divine, and supporting each other on the journey. The mission of BREATHE, from the community website, states: "As people created for community, and through our dependence on the living God, we seek to inspire the imagination, refresh the soul, and nurture the body, all within the context of deep, interdependent relationships."

The process of emerging has never stopped. In the spring of 2005, BREATHE launched a website designed to connect, inform, and inspire people from all walks of life. This too has continued to take shape and evolve. Many people near and far have made use of the online chat rooms, message boards, photo galleries, information pages, Pay Pal method of contributing or tithing, prayer posts, and attractive communication in order to be supported, give support, or simply find out how to connect with BREATHE.

As a small home-based faith community, it is our conviction that all that we are and do is to be a compliment to God. Our worship is not just for a few hours on Sunday and perhaps the occasional Wednesday night. All of our days, decisions and hopes, our lively conversations and humdrum Tuesday afternoons, everything, is an expression of worship. We want to live with a sense of the eternal. Whenever we gather together or are on our own, we know that there is a whole lot more going on than we realize. The supernatural is near. In light of that, when we set aside time to appreciate and give God the highest compliment, we have seen it as a continuation of our daily lives—our eating, and laughing, thinking, talking, singing, dancing, watching, praying, greeting, walking, wondering, stillness, garbage-gathering, serving, contributing, reading, everything we do, even our breathing, is an expression of thoughtful gratitude. We believe, as Neil Cole states, that "church should happen wherever life happens. You shouldn't have to leave life to go to church."[3]

When the home-based faith community gathers for Inhale, the Sunday morning worship experience, there is a sense of freedom and comfort that evokes honesty and authenticity with each other and with God. Congregating in a home has the feel of a house party, a celebration, or a large Thanksgiving family meal. On these occasions and in this environment, those who gather as the BREATHE community openly and willingly talk about their daily experiences and share the stories of their lives. It is our sense that worship is about noticing what God is doing in each others' lives. Describing that activity is part of the process of worship. When we appreciate the involvement that God has in our lives personally and corporately, our thoughtfulness becomes thankfulness and finally a narrative of worship.

It is our conviction, along with Herbert Anderson and Edward Foley, that:

> Like other human rituals, worship is neither just an exercise in divine data distribution nor a rehearsal of celestial rules. Rather, public worship is a significant, even indispensable way for believers to exercise and acquire faith. It is a way in which believers discover how God is or can be a part of their lives. Worship is also an important medium for discovering the significance that belief in God has for the way one shapes personal relationships or conducts worldly affairs. Worship is a critical exercise in meaning-making for believers...public worship cannot enable the human-divine encounter without adequate attention to narrative. In particular, sacred rituals must respect and balance human stories—both individual and communal—with the divine narrative without manipulation or deceit.[4]

As we gather over a creatively tasty brunch, sitting and standing in the living/dining room, we talk and we tell the stories of our lives. Eventually the group will make its way to the family room that is comfortably furnished and decorated. Here, we continue our talking and worship as one of us (usually myself) facilitates various spiritual practices. Because we value flexibility, what may be planned and what actually happens can look quite different. Interruptions are welcome if God is directing the experience.

Usually we will have a time of silence in order to slow down, reflect on the scriptural command to, "Be still and know that I am God" (Isaiah 46:10), and to practice listening. Images and music may accompany the stillness, or perhaps nothing but the rhythm of our breathing can be heard. The atmosphere is always very relaxed—regular coffee refills abound—though earnest in devotion. The BREATHE community enjoys worshipping through such practices as listening to music, singing, going for walks along the western dyke of Richmond, discussing teaching and music videos, reading and thinking about Scripture, watching movies, drawing, painting, writing, consuming and remembering by means of the Eucharist, telling our stories and praying.

Although our authentic worship, intimate community, and spiritual nurture have resonated with those who draw together, many questions have continued to capture my attention, especially as I explore the spiritual formation practices of other nascent faith communities. Are people actually growing in their spiritual lives? Do the burgeoning community and the communal experiences afford people the opportunity for spiritual growth? Do our spiritual practices nurture spiritual formation? All of those questions were in the back of my mind as we continued to meet, grow, and weave together our spiritual and practical lives.

The following study is the result of those questions, the desire to be changed by our experiences with the Divine, and the journey that we are privileged to travel with God. It is not our desire to have a form of godliness (ritual, spiritual practices) while ignoring or denying the power (God's transforming presence). BREATHE's fundamental conviction is that God is to be experienced, and that we are changed by that experience. Or as Hebrews 11:6 states, "And without faith it is impossible to please Him, for he who comes to God must believe that He is and that He is a rewarder of those who seek Him."

The Gospel and Culture

Breathing is essential and basic to human growth. And spiritual growth is no different. For the BREATHE community this means 'inhaling' (communal worship) and 'exhaling' (intersecting culture and faith). While Inhale generally involves an opportunity to appreciate life and God, Exhale is an open invitation to connect one's worldview, ideas, culture and wonder in a familiar setting – the pub. Every other Tuesday night, some of the BREATHE community gather at the Elephant & Castle Restaurant & Pub in their 'upper room' known as The Sandbar, to relax, nourish our physical appetite with good food and beverages, and to examine our world, faith, and lives. Exhale is held in a culturally popular setting and often attracts more people who have no use for church but who are on speaking terms with God, than those who are followers of Jesus. From time to time, even patrons and employees of the Pub will join in on the conversation and share their stories.

"I enjoy coming to these Tuesday nights, you all disagree so agreeably," commented Wade, a regular at Exhale. The opportunity to take an hour or two after a long day and simply unwind, all the while getting your thoughts and honest feelings out and perhaps understand a bit more about social issues, society, faith, etc., has clearly resonated with so many. The drop-in nature of Exhale means that no one is sure who will be there from week to week, but the discussions, if not informative and enlightening, are always personal and...cathartic. Our BREATHE community has become very close to many of the staff and management at the Elephant and Castle, and from the hugs, waves and smiles, it's evident that we mutually look forward to seeing each other every second Tuesday.

"I have nowhere else in my life where I'm able to spend some time like this with such a variety of people to discuss life," revealed Ian who struggles to get to Exhale due to work, but who passionately and desperately enjoys the gathering. In a sense, Exhale offers a place to be yourself and gain some perspective. And that is something that we have found is lacking in our culture and to which many will go to great lengths to experience. From Vancouver to Burnaby to White Rock and Surrey, people come by bus, car and bike as often as their schedule will allow them. Exhale is not an evangelical sleight-of-hand or an attempt to be cool and alternative (whatever that means). We just enjoy being ourselves together, welcoming new conversationalists, and trying to understand the best kind of life.

Connecting our faith and culture is not limited to the engaging gatherings on Tuesday nights at Exhale. In fact culturally redemptive experiences occur frequently as each person from the community lives his or her faith, however strong or struggling it may be. From seemingly benign conversations at Starbucks to dialogue over a Saturday morning run, the line between culture and Christianity is erased. God becomes part of the fabric of our everyday lives. Our best intentions on Sundays as we Inhale are to love God. "In loving me you made me loving," asserted Augustine, and for the BREATHE community, that love is experienced through some common practice.

Common Meal. The emerging faith community of BREATHE regularly experiences hospitality in the form of the common meal. Our worship incorporates eating in community and celebrating the goodness and faithfulness of God. The common meal as we practice it comes in two forms: Brunch – a diverse and delicious, cold and hot, help-yourself meal that replaces breakfast and lunch and is not only amazingly tasty but healthy as well; and Communion/Eucharist – taking and eating food and drink that is intended to remind participants of the broken and bleeding body of Jesus.

It is our belief that all our eating and drinking can remind us of our finiteness and Christ's sacrifice on our behalf. At times, however, it is helpful and necessary to set apart a specific experience in order to better focus our attention. Brunch happens every week, while Communion/ Eucharist may happen once a month or once every six to eight weeks.

Eating and experiencing hospitality in this way is an expression of community and unity. As Christians, our theological basis for hospitality is Creation. Creation is the ultimate expression of God's hospitality to his creatures.

God's creation gives us a model for making and sharing homes with people, but the reality of God's Trinitarian life suggests that Christian hospitality goes further than that. We are not meant simply to invite people into our homes, but also to invite them into our lives. Having guests and visitors, if we do it right, is not an imposition, because we are not meant to rearrange our lives for our guests: we are meant to invite our guests to enter into our lives as they are. It is this forging of relationships that transforms entertaining (i.e., deadly dull cocktail parties at the country club) into hospitality (i.e., a simple pizza on my floor).[5]

Teacher, author and biblical Hebrew scholar, Douglas A. Wheeler, states:

> The manner in which the first-century Christians shared their meals was part of a rich Jewish cultural tradition that has by and large been lost to modern Christianity. The first believers celebrated mealtime in the tradition of Bircath Hamazon (called "benching"), a time for family celebration, fellowship, and worship around the table that had come to be seen as an altar. The early believers not only knew, but also applied the biblical truth that "man does not live by bread alone, but by every word that travels out of the mouth of the Lord" (Deuteronomy 8:3). An empty stomach has a disturbing effect on the mind and interferes with the concentration of thought. Thus, the meal was not something to be rushed through, but a time to be enjoyed. Mealtime was a time when something spiritual, something special was produced. It was also a time when people talked about their day, their experiences, their work, their struggles…what makes them laugh. Basically as we eat and talk with and to each other we share not only the food that God provides (bringing a realization that we are dependent on Him) but also our very lives.[6]

Implicatory Dialogue. The notion of dialogue is not foreign to spiritual groups or worshipers. Over the centuries, the social, dynamic, and theological process of dialoging about faith, truth, and life has been commonplace, both formally and informally. The perspective of implication over application, however, is an experience that is being rejuvenated by Doug Pagitt, pastor of Solomon's Porch in Minneapolis, Minnesota.

There is a fine yet significant difference between application—the buzzword of the past century—and implication, the intuitive meta-narrative from outside time. Application is about how a piece of information fits into your life. Implication is not about fitting; it's about redefining. It's not a value-added suggestion; it's a call to see the story

73

and join in it... The practice of applying Scripture to our lives is not the established Christian tradition but rather the product of more recent ways of thinking about church. Our post-Enlightenment ways of thinking move us to want answers rather than more questions, to seek instant take-away rather than long processes, to seek out solutions rather than ponder the problem itself.[7]

Progressive implicatory dialogue is where the content of the presentation is established in the context of a healthy relationship between the presenter and the listeners, and substantive changes in the content are then created as a result of this relationship.

The ability to take a nugget of truth (information) from Scripture and rub it on our lives in such a way that we utilize it, has been a priority in preaching and churches for many years. For followers of Jesus it has become our default mode of making Scripture practical. The essential disconnect with this form of integration is that it is individualistic and usually judgmental. The question in application usually rests on "I": "Do you see what I see?" or "Do you know what I know?" And this process is reinforced by a preacher or leader who seeks to make that application to everyone in earshot regardless of the diversity we possess as people. Application has a sense of "me" to it; implication has a sense of "us." As Doug Pagitt explains,

> This difference is crucial to the ways in which we understand ourselves as God's people. Application allows us to remain disconnected, to think of our faith in individualistic terms. But nowhere in the Bible do we see faith as an individual endeavor. It is always a communal practice. Even the stories about people of faith —Moses, David, Job—are told from a communal perspective; the point is never what happens to them but what happens because of them. The sense of us that comes through implication opens our communities to the notion that we aren't simply people who gather once a week for a common experience, but we are part of something bigger than ourselves. Suddenly, we tap into the power of the community to be a source of formation, of life change. Implication takes down the walls that exist between the people in our communities and allows us to be vulnerable with one another as we share in the journey of faith. It moves us to connect with other people who have been down this road. Think about the ways in which the disciples responded whenever they listened to Jesus

preach. They wondered what this call would mean for them. They talked to each other about what they'd heard. They asked Jesus questions about how his words were changing them. They were not asking questions of application, but of reorientation.[8]

It would be tempting to think of implicatory dialogue as simply discussion. However, as mentioned above, while implicatory dialogue may appear discussion-like, the content or perspective is uniquely different. Implicatory dialogue is talking about God's life in us as a community.

During Inhale, our conversation and interaction is a time where the community is implicated by the story of God, becoming part of it and arranging our lives around it. The content for these discussions, for this study, came from the weekly use of the Nooma[9] video series (numbers 1-5, 7, 8,10,11).

Contemplative Prayer. The BREATHE community seeks to practice contemplative prayer in order to be fully present or "at home" with God. Thomas Green speaks about the experience of contemplative prayer and says:

> There is a newfound joy simply in being still in the presence of the Lord, just as good friends find joy simply in being together. They are not self-conscious or nervous about silences. They don't plan their conversation or analyze their relationship. They don't really "think about" each other much when they are together. They just are, and they are happy to be together, whatever may be happening. Talking and silence are spontaneous and easy and relaxed – not laboured or artificial.[10]

Each week the BREATHE community engages in a particular aspect of contemplative prayer from the following:

- Intercessory prayer – prayers made on behalf of someone else.
- Body prayer – using body posture and physical actions to connect with God and communicate desire.
- Prayer-walking – talking to God while walking in His creation.
- Silence and Solitude – being still and quiet in God's presence in order to listen.

Creative Arts. When we consciously attend to an object, especially an art object, we will have some kind of reaction to it. The response may be subtle or it may be strong; it may be positive or negative. We may be turned off, aroused, repulsed, delighted, or disappointed; we may be moved to tears, frightened, bored, or baffled. Our responses may be different from those of the person next to us. But no matter how we respond, we are slightly or significantly different for having had the viewing, or the hearing – for having paid attention. Our memories, even our ideas, are essentially constructed out of images and colours, spatial relationships, smells, sensations, and sounds, more than they are made of words ordered into sentences – even when we record and transmit them this way.

Therefore, for the arts to enable a worship experience, we must give up the familiarity of the status quo (whether comforting or stifling) and take a chance on the unknown.[11] To risk the gaze into the creative unknown is to not only encounter the very nature of God (creative Creator), but realize that the thing we see is not the truth itself but a means for our encounter with the Truth. "But we all, with unveiled face, beholding as in a mirror the glory of the Lord, are being transformed into the same image from glory to glory, just as from the Lord, the Spirit."[12] Each week during Inhale, we engage in a particular aspect of the creative arts from the following:

- Music and Technology – facilitating singing and thought by using visual PowerPoint slides together with pre-recorded music from various genres.
- Writing – creating written expressions of worship through prayers, poems, letters, songs, thoughts about God.
- Drawing and Painting – creating visual expressions of worship through sketching or Buddha Board paintings.

Common Practices

"In many ways," states Oliver Davies, "Christianity lives by its ability to rediscover its past." Davies goes on to say: "The history of Christianity shows a constant tendency toward invigorating revival and rediscovery of its roots as well as to polemics surrounding the varying definitions of tradition. The way to appropriate traditions from the past, originally practiced in social and spiritual contexts very different from our own, is problematic."[13]

Our faith is a historically rich and culturally diverse faith that has gone through vast changes and cycles of experience and renewal. Nevertheless, one value of studying the accustomed practices of early faith communities is that they alert us to possibilities of Christian existence and formation which are both ancient and new.

The spiritual formation practices of the BREATHE community are rooted in history. As I have discussed above, from the early church notions of community, home-based gathering, and participatory style to the Benedictine and Celtic practices of prayer, lectio divina, silence, hospitality, and poetry, there is a thread of common connection to our current spiritual community. BREATHE is joined, present to the past, through similar spiritual formation practices and methods of connecting with God.

Although the specific form of spiritual practice does not mirror the historic form exactly, the connection is clear. Benedictine and Celtic Christians gathered in monasteries or circular-walled villages in order to devote themselves to encountering and serving God. Their gatherings included everyday life experiences – eating, talking, thinking, and working. From these come the BREATHE practices of the common meal and implicatory dialogue. The quest for the Divine caused early Christians to engage in various forms of meditation, contemplation, and prayer as well as reading and writing about Scripture. Here again, the BREATHE practices of contemplative prayer and the creative arts are linked.

The BREATHE community in many ways has rediscovered its past. The rich heritage of spiritual formation practices of the first to eighth centuries has enriched and renewed the small home-based faith community of BREATHE in the 21st century.

About Phil Harbridge

Phil Harbridge was a youth pastor for 25 years. He completed his Master of Divinity at Denver Seminary, Colorado. Phil has pastored in

Denver, Kitchener/Waterloo, and Vancouver. Most recently he completed his Doctor of Ministry from Carey Theological College. "Dr. Phil" is an avid runner, marathoner, and triathlete. He and his wife Kay, have two grown daughters.

Bibliography

Anderson, Herbert, and Edward Foley, *Mighty Stories, Dangerous Rituals: Weaving Together the Human and the Divine.* San Francisco: Jossey-Bass, 1998.

City of Richmond. "Richmond." No pages. Online: http:// www.richmond.ca/home.htm.

Cole, Neil. *Organic Church: Growing Faith Where Life Happens.* San Francisco: Jossey-Bass, 2005.

Davies, Oliver. *The Creativity of God: World, Eucharist, Reason.* Cambridge: Cambridge University Press, 2005.

Green, S.J., Thomas H. *When the Well Runs Dry: Prayer Beyond the Beginnings.* Notre Dame: Ave Maria, 1998.

Jensen, Robin M. *The Substance of Things Seen: Art, Faith, and the Christian Community.* Grand Rapids: William B. Eerdmans Publishing, 2004.

Pagitt, Doug. *Preaching Re-Imagined: The Role of the Sermon in Communities of Faith.* Grand Rapids: Zondervan, 2003.

Taylor, Steve. *The Out of Bounds Church? Learning to Create a Community of Faith in a Culture of Change.* Grand Rapids: Zondervan/Youth Specialties, 2005.

Winner, Lauren F. *Mudhouse Sabbath: An Invitation to a Life of Spiritual Discipline.* Brewster: Paraclette, 2003.

---

1 Taylor, *The Out of Bounds Church?,* 81.

2 City of Richmond, "Richmond."

3 Cole, *Organic Church,* 24.

4 Anderson and Foley, *Mighty Stories, Dangerous Rituals,* 42-43.

5 Winner, *Mudhouse Sabbath,* 46-47.

6 Restoration Foundation. (website no longer active.)

7 Pagitt, *Preaching Re-Imagined,* 97, 102.

8 Ibid., 99-100.

9 http://www.nooma.com. We can get anything we want, from anywhere in the world, whenever we want it. That's how it is and that's how we want it to be. Still, our lives aren't any different than other generations before us. Our time is different. We want spiritual direction, but it has to be real for us and available when we need it. NOOMA works: short films with communicators that really speak to us.

10 Green, *When the Well Runs Dry*, 51.

11 Jensen, *The Substance of Things Seen*, 3.

12 2 Corinthians 3:18.

13 Davies, *The Creativity of God*, 24-25.

Chapter 4

Downtown Windsor Community Cooperative, Windsor

Robert Cameron

Margo, my wife, and I moved back home to the downtown of Windsor, Ontario, in September 2010. For the previous 20 years, we had lived and worked in the Greater Toronto Area, where our experiences in the Chartwell Baptist Church community shaped the decision to return home to Windsor as missionaries. Our four daughters chose to return with them and are currently in high school and the University of Windsor.

Downtown Windsor Community Cooperative is an experiment in the Church's creative engagement with the culture in a post-Christendom, urban, Canadian setting. We are a community of missionaries working for the renewal of the city through rebuilding neighbourhood communities. We are committed to exploring how the Body of Christ loves God, one another, and our neighbours from "Monday to Saturday." Our presupposition is that the community modeled in the middle of the everyday life of the neighbourhood is the greatest apologetic for the gospel. The challenge is that our individualistic middle-class culture has lost much of our understanding and practice of community.

Our objective is to establish a "lighthouse" – a missionary community – in every neighbourhood of the parish, serving as a sign, foretaste, and instrument of the Kingdom of Heaven. Each Lighthouse initiates development projects and extends hospitality to its neighbours. Periodically, all those involved in the mission of DWCC gather to encourage one another and realign themselves to the mission. DWCC has an integrative approach around the three relationships – Lighthouses, Community Development, and Gathering. All three provide engagement between the Church and the world, spiritual formation, and entry into the Christ Community.

The parish of Downtown Windsor is four square kilometers of 16,000 persons living in a couple dozen neighbourhoods. It is diverse in terms of income, ethnicity, and housing. It is a walkable city with a solid representation of business, cultural and educational opportunities. The city was hit hard by the downturn in the automotive industry and has one of the highest unemployment rates in Canada. Like a depression in the city landscape, there is a disproportionately large number of hurting persons – mental health issues, addictions, and poverty – who live in the city centre to access social services. Within the density of the parish, affluence and poverty, stability and transiency, doctors and drug addicts, live side by side.

Our vision is the adoption and contextualizing of God's vision for the City – that Windsor is "a good place to grow up and a good place to grow old." Speaking through the prophet Zechariah, God paints a picture of a city transformed by his presence. "Old men and old women will come back to Jerusalem, sit on benches on the streets and spin tales, move around safely with their canes—a good city to grow old in. And boys and girls will fill the public parks, laughing and playing—a good city to grow up in."[1]

Our calling as a Collaborative is to participate with God in the realization of this vision. We regularly ask ourselves, "What would it look like if God moved into this particular neighbourhood? What do we bring that would create an environment of safety for the elderly and the children and for all vulnerable people who live in the parish?"

The ongoing relational shift between the gospel and culture requires that we explore a new way of engaging and understanding our role and purpose of the Church in this country. No longer the centre of spiritual authority nor the wielder of moral power, the Church needs to live as one of many voices, with humility, and as a participant with others in loving our neighbours. Our model and ministry becomes the validation of that message.

This includes seeing ourselves as participants with God in his work of reconciliation. The mission is to serve and bless the city rather than to rule within it, or live apart from it. Second Corinthians 5:16-20 describes our mandate and activity. As ambassadors of the Kingdom of Heaven, we are to model a counterculture. This is a culture that loves each other based on the principles and practices of Jesus. The model presents a living picture of what it means to live in harmony with others based on love and servanthood.

The ministry of reconciliation is our activity. If reconciliation is restoring that which is broken to its original purpose, then we are participants in the process of knitting people together – to God, to one another, and within themselves. Modeling a community of Jesus coupled with words and actions that encourage reconciliation, becomes a living illustration making sense of the message of reconciliation. Our words clarify our actions. Our actions create a curiosity and a benevolent perplexity; they beg an explanation.

In the context of downtown Windsor our mission is to pursue renewal of the city through building neighbourhood community. Factors affecting the deterioration of the city have been population flight from the urban centre, poor planning that has been a solvent to neighbourhood spirit, and the flight of the churches to the suburbs.

Within each walkable neighbourhood we see two overlapping communities developing. At the core is a community of Christ-followers who live in the neighbourhood. We identify Christians already present on the block, realign them to a missionary mindset, and draw them together as a community of mutual care, while turning their hearts outward to include their neighbours.

The second community is the parish: a neighbourhood that includes everyone living on the block. Based on the principles of Asset-Based Community Development (www.abundantcommunity.org), the gifts and leadership necessary to resolve the problems and realize the hopes of a street are already exist within it. Leveraging the first community's servant-mindedness, this broader community is encouraged through activism and leadership development toward the neighbourhood's wellbeing. For the Church to be a participant within the larger community requires it to relocate and identify with the parish, or redefine its purpose for why its people already live on the street.

Strategically implementing this model requires three hubs:

- A Lighthouse in every neighbourhood,
- Community development activities, and
- Gathering regularly to realign to the mission.

Lighthouses

We open their home up each Thursday night for friends and neighbours to come for potluck supper together, spiritual formation, plan and update their community development. Supporting our family are several persons who don't live in the neighbourhood but are committed to the mission and provide healthy friendship for the Lighthouse community. The Lighthouse organizes the volunteers for the local elementary school's breakfast club which ensures all children begin the day on a full stomach. Each night that we gather, we update and encourage the volunteers and consider further ways of caring for our neighbourhood's wellbeing.

A Lighthouse is that core Christian community that serves a particular neighbourhood. The leadership of each Lighthouse resides on the street. Their residence is the physical presence where the core community regularly meets to pray, eat, and love one another. This core team is supported by friends who associate regularly with the group, committed to supporting them in their engagement of the mission.

Currently a Lighthouse seems to move through five stages of formation. The first is leadership moving into and identifying with a neighbourhood. Second is establishing a team consisting of people outside the DWCC supportive of the mission and willing to pray weekly for specific needs and people. The second is bringing two additional persons to do life as friends in the neighbourhood, and who hang around enough to be identified by neighbours as their acquaintances and developing friends. The third is acts of hospitality that regularly bring neighbours together into a growing relationship of trust. The fourth is a pattern of discipleship that walks with neighbours in their journey towards walking with Jesus. And the fifth is taking a Lighthouse into a new neighbourhood to birth a new Lighthouse.

Within each Lighthouse are relational triads of accountability. Our pattern is John 11 and the raising of Lazarus. After rescuing him from the tomb, Jesus instructed his friends and family to remove the grave clothes. In the trusting relationship of three, we find a safe place to explore throwing off those things that inhibit our movement in the resurrection life.

A derivation of the Lighthouse is our Men's and Women's Intentional Community Houses. Each home is run by three persons who commit to life together while making space for two additional residents in transition. Through faith and friendship they create a home for healing and restoration. Costs and responsibilities are shared by all residents. The healing process is framed by brief solution-therapy models. Each home is also responsible for a wider mission: to engage its neighbourhood, making it a better place in which to grow up and grow old.

Community Development

Each neighbourhood's needs and possibilities vary. The demographic makeup, existing organizations, and gifts of the residents shape the needs. Currently, a common theme running through many of the neighbourhoods is food security. DWCC mobilizes the residents to organize and plant local gardens with accessible, nutritious and affordable foods. The hidden purpose is to bring neighbours together and move them from strangers to acquaintances to friends. As the garden team grows, leaders are identified, Christians residing on the street are brought together, and a grassroots leadership team develops. The leaders begin to dream about different challenges that would renew their neighbourhood. The core Christian community encourages and supports their leadership in these issues.

Neighbourhood-centred development functions at many levels. Each activity, such as breakfast clubs or community gardens, holds some benefit for the residents. They also provide an avenue for relational engagement: a common place for meeting neighbours, working together on a common cause, and developing friendships. Through these interactions we meet other Christians and can begin conversations about them joining us in extending the core Christ community.

Gathering

The scattering effect of sending persons on mission can lead to the air coming out of the missional balloon. Through our weekday interactions we hear stories of lament and celebration that need to be shared with those who 'understand us' and to corporately offer them to God as prayers of lament and complaint, gratitude and worship. The mission is the strong thread woven through our gatherings. During the Gathering we reflect on the week of mission, and bring our scattered experiences together to discern God's mission in the context of the downtown.

Participants in DWCC attend several different congregations on Sunday mornings. However, our leadership meets together once a month for a few hours, enjoying a meal together, sharing stories, communion, and a directed conversation. Participation is by invitation as we wrestle through the implications of a covenant, and what we are learning about the model through our experiences.

As we grow in numbers and activities, gathering becomes vitally important for keeping the mission from scattering us and drifting from the mission. Our practices seem to be coalescing around three palettes:

- First, storytelling gives a chance for all persons to share their experiences whether laments or celebrations. Either in triads or in our full gathering the stories are part of our offering to God. Our prayers are shaped by the story, laments or praises.
- Second, the three ritual commands of the Lord (Communion, Baptism, Footwashing) are being explored for their place in our community. We celebrate the Lord's Supper every time we gather. In the meal we share together we continue our stories of ministry remembering the Lord in his mission; in breaking bread and drinking wine we break down denominational boundaries, united in our common vision.
- Third, we seek to rediscover the disciplines of Church Calendar, *Lectio Divina*, and Divine Hours. Because we focus less than five percent of our time on Gathering we are seeking

ways to simplify the planning while maintaining its importance. By using the Church Lectionary we trust the Spirit to direct our Scripture reading and tether our creative endeavours to the history of the Church.

Last summer Brian asked if he could be baptized. We talked about what baptism signifies and in his simplicity Brian understood most of it, but not all. Baptism got in his craw and he persisted in his determination. We celebrated last August on a Thursday evening. Our supper group marched down the street to a neighbour's pool – piquing the curiosity of all the neighbours between our two houses – and baptized him. We talked about how baptism is staking a claim: I identify with Jesus and his followers, and I will adjust my behaviour by fine-tuning my sensitivity to Jesus' call and presence.

Spiritual Formation in the Heat of Mission

A missional spirituality is a set of beliefs and practices that nurture a growing awareness and enjoyment of the dance that God draws us into in his mission of reconciling the world. Formation occurs by participating with, and in the presence of, the Trinity. A missional spirituality will tune the frequency of our spirit to see and sense the presence and calling of God on us and those around us.

Critical to perseverance in the mission is a spirituality that sustains the individual and the community. Formative disciplines are the means to the end of experiencing the presence of the Lord. They attune our spirit to the frequency of God, move us to obedience, restore our souls, alert us to the presence of God, and enrich our enjoyment of his company. It is not a passive private practice. God is active in the world around us and calls us into the fray. Likewise the movement of the world towards God does not necessarily begin in a church-building setting. Rather, if the Spirit is active in the world (John 16:8-11), then formation is taking place in the workplace, on the sidewalks, and "third places."

Spiritual Formation in Four Spaces

Formative practices for the DWCC fall into four quadrants – mountain and border, personal and corporate. God is not only drawing us as persons to a richer experience of the Trinity, but the corporate body of the Church as well. In all spaces we need to become attuned to hearing and obeying the voice of the Lord. Missional Spirituality has to be flexible enough so that in the midst of an interaction such as in the marketplace, we are able to discern where the Kingdom of God is breaking in, and how the Lord invites us to participate with ministry and message.

Borderlands.[2] In Acts 8 the relationship between the Spirit, Philip, and the Ethiopian describe the engagement of mission. Philip is obedient to the Spirit and the experience becomes energizing and empowering. We are formed and nourished through seeing God at work, responding to his invitation to enter in, and reflecting on the experience in prayer. Adventure with God is fluid, spontaneous, and re-members us, re-connects us with the presence of God in our neighbourhoods.

Mountaintop. On the mountain we meet God in solitude and silence. It is the place of intimacy and timelessness where we go to be absent from the world's pulls and demands. It is the experience of the encounter with the Divine as we bring our interaction with the world to the Father. We pine for the lover's time alone in the presence of the Trinity, and to gather corporately as the Body of Christ gathers at the table of the Lord.

Rhythms & Practices	Mountaintop Practices (Stepping away for meeting with Jesus)	Borderlands Engagement Practices (Meeting the Spirit in the world)
Personal	• Sabbath. • Private Devotion. • Divine Hours. • *Examen* or Prayerful reflection. • *Lectio Divina* or Scripture reflection.	•Hospitality. • Presence through zigzagging. • Presence through setting rhythms of life for engagement (work, shopping, and play). • Conversational Prayer.
Corporate/ Community	**The Gathering** • Singing. • Scripture/Lectionary Reading. • Teaching (fine-tuning the mission). • Listening Prayer. • Sharing our stories. • Baptism and Footwashing. • Communion and a Shared Meal.	**Community Development** • Loving Mercy. • Doing Justice. • Building Relationships.

The church down the street called. Dave was attending their weekday Bible Study and seemed to be homeless, in need of some assistance. Dave and I went out for coffee, and he began to slowly unfold a story filled with amnesia-like symptoms; he was perplexed about who he was. As the weeks went by we found out that Dave was a highly-skilled mechanic. He fixed my car and helped folks with repairs. As we spent time together we gleaned bits of the story. Dave made a conscious decision to follow Jesus that summer; he asked a lot of questions on certainty, forgiveness of deep past sins, and fear of God's disapproval.

As the summer moved along things didn't add up in Dave's story, even as he developed rhythms of prayer and study and reflection and a distorted fixation on fasting. One afternoon with Jim, whom he trusted as a grandfather, the truth was confronted. Dave was from Detroit. He had come across the border, sold his car, ditched his identity, and began to recreate himself as a Canadian. We confronted him and he ran away as fast as he could. I feared we had lost him and betrayed him.

Two weeks later Dave showed up on the front porch. We sat in the kitchen and he answered all my questions, and eventually got on the phone and called his family. In the next room he established contact as the prodigal son; he apologized and asked his parents for their forgiveness. We cried as we listened in around the corner as his parents accepted their lost son back. Within hours his sister was at our house and embraced her brother. Dave calls every other week to check in and see how his friends are doing. He got his old job back, and found a church that is willing to answer all his questions with patience.

We were sorry to see Dave leave. So much had been invested in him and he had become a friend (plus he could fix almost anything around the house). But we realize his story is a gift from God as a living parable of the Good News. God is at work reconciling the world to himself through Jesus. Reconciliation is putting things back together the way they're meant to be. And we as the Church are called out and drawn together to be participants in that reconciliation through models, messengers and ministers. Dave's restoration to family and identity is the reconciling work of God in restoring what was marred. We were privileged to be in on the work.

In the context of our parish, reconciliation takes place on numerous levels. God is interested in them all. We seek to reconcile neighbours alienated through violence and danger in 920 Ouellette; or newcomers from other countries who arrive as aliens become integrated into our community; or for that matter anyone alienated from the Kingdom of Heaven. So many need healing: people shattered by addictions, and people unable to use their hands or minds in useful work or any sense of productive livelihood.

As I write this, Leslie Pilgrim is in our home's ping pong room with several children and one of their fathers. They all live in an under-resourced neighbourhood, and our basement and backyard trampoline are a Saturday treat for them. Up to a year ago Leslie was homeless, controlled by addictions that assuaged the brokenness and wounds of his past. The Spirit miraculously transformed and rescued him from violence and alienation. A restorative work began in him that knit him back into community, empowering him to choose wisely. Living in a boarding house, one step up from his homelessness, he ministers to those he can easily identify with, and announces the good news of Jesus. Earlier this week he committed to relocate into a troubled housing project and serve as an incarnational missionary.

Through compassion and advocacy Leslie cares for others and brings them into the Community of Christ. An unpolished evangelist, maybe not unlike Peter, his impact can be measured by a continuously growing number of developing followers of Jesus. As participants in reconciliation Leslie moves strangers and enemies to acquaintance and friendship, and ultimately to becoming fellow followers of Jesus. His ministry of reconciliation is the Good News in action, and his message becomes the explanation for the acts of love and kindness.

Pursuing hospitality – Countering the individualistic mindset

When the doorbell rang and Kelso barked we knew it was someone new at the front door. Kelso, our golden retriever, knows the regulars and the strangers even before the door opens. It was 9:30 p.m., dark, cold and raining. Dave was on the porch with a bag full of an assortment of library books on philosophy and computer sciences. Mental illness has reshaped his life after an extensive career as a courier and janitor. He has the financial wherewithal but is unwilling to live almost anywhere but on the streets. "Dave, good to see you. Come on in out of the rain." He quickly accepted the additional offer of some supper. Sitting together at the kitchen table, he devoured the leftovers from our family dinner. We chatted for a while, mostly us listening to his meandering train of thought, mostly providing friendship and dignity. When Dave left he was heading to a coffee shop that lets him stay most of the night. What was I thinking by not sending him to the Rivers Edge (our Men's Community House) for a dry and warm couch?

I find soup kitchens sloppy seconds of the sacred meal. Providing a service, they're a friendless but efficient dispersal of food for the body but a poor source of calories for the soul. We understand the Trinity as a community of three Persons in whom their love for one another spills over to their creation to come and join them at the dinner table of fellowship. Our dining room tables are a sacred place that echo the Trinity's invitation. We sit with them as friendly servants enjoying their company and extending grace and dignity as friends, blurring the line between care provider and client.

Dave's visit was unexpected. Alternatively, on Thursday evenings we open our door formally to whomever can walk to our house and enjoy a potluck meal together. Brian brings the freshie sticks and makes the drink; Leo brings odd things that have a high probability of being shoplifted on his way through the grocery store. Jason peels the potatoes; Jenny takes over control of the kitchen's early shift. Over the weeks these strangers of all sorts become friends learning to care for one another. It is theology in action, an apologetic for the Trinity, an application of grace and love.

About Bob Cameron

Bob and Margo Cameron live in downtown Windsor with their four daughters. They grew up in Windsor and attended the U of W where Margo completed her B.Sc. Nursing. Two years into their marriage they moved to Mississauga-Oakville to expand their family-owned Christian bookstores. They were actively involved in ministry and leadership at Chartwell Baptist Church. After leaving the business Bob served for several years as community pastor at Chartwell Mississauga and completed his In Ministry MDiv at Tyndale Seminary. In the fall of 2010 they were sent as missionaries to downtown Windsor by Chartwell through Vision Ministries Canada.

Bibliography

Nelson, Gary. *Borderland Churches: A Congregation's Introduction to Missional Living.* St. Louis: Chalice, 2009.

---

1 Zechariah 8:4-5. The Message.

2 Nelson, *Borderland Churches.*

Chapter 5

Treasure in Jars of Clay: Freedom Vineyard, Ottawa
Frank Emanuel

I (Len) was in conversation with Frank one day when he learned of
Fresh and Re:Fresh. As we talked it hit me that his community would
be a good one to run through the grid developed by the authors of
Treasure in Jars of Clay: Patterns of Missional Faithfulness, which was
the follow-on work to the outstanding Missional Church. Treasure in
Jars of Clay is not a "how-to" book, but rather addresses the question,
"How would you know a missional church if you saw one?" It also
encourages communities of faith that are in transition. What in the life
of a church indicates that it is missional? How can communities find
the courage to move toward being more outward oriented?

The second book began by taking the twelve indicators of a missional
church that grew out of the first book, and then asking people across
North America to nominate congregations that fit the indicators. In the
process the authors discovered that these indicators were not adequate.
Secondly, they realized that none of the indicators had to do with
leaders, yet authority within the congregation was a key factor in the
movement toward becoming missional. Finally, the authors realized that

what they had were not indicators, but "patterns." The result was the identification of eight patterns of missional faithfulness.

Despite our best intentions of planting a traditional Vineyard church, we have taken to calling Freedom Vineyard the "alternative" Vineyard of Ottawa. Our community has been gathering, in a variety of settings, locations and forms, since the fall of 2001. Our parent church is River City Vineyard in Sarnia, about seven hours away, so even from the beginning we have been pretty much on our own. We met first as a group of believers who were less than satisfied with our experiences in various local congregations. We set out to run a six-month trial; we decided that if we were growing spiritually after this period then we had a good case for planting a new church. After that time we were excited to open the group up and see what would happen.

We planted Freedom at a time when the dust was settling on a particularly tumultuous chapter of the Vineyard's history. The expectations of the renewal culture, after the Toronto Blessing, proved to be difficult for many Vineyard churches. The original Ottawa Vineyard church, which some of us had been part of, had fallen apart in the aftermath of this mixed blessing. In practical terms, gone were the days when calling yourself a Vineyard garnered you an instant congregation.

As a result, we spent a lot of the early years figuring out what was actually working and what was not. All of us felt strongly that Ottawa needed the unique contribution a Vineyard could offer, but we were less prepared for the actual contribution that Freedom Vineyard would make. As church planters, we took a passion for equipping, stirred in a vibrant love of the encounter of God, and we honestly expected a traditional Vineyard to emerge. However, what emerged is not your traditional Vineyard church. Certainly Freedom has Vineyard values in its heart, but the form our church grew into is completely different from what any of us had experienced before.

The Journey to Where We Are

We started out with a half dozen people who all had a positive history with the Vineyard. Numbers is always an odd game for us because at any given time you can count on an active core of about a dozen folk that you can not scare off (believe me, in some cases we have tried), and at the same time a much larger sphere of influence in our city, both inside and outside of the Christian Church. Over the years this sphere of influence has grown beyond the borders of our city. The Freedom groups that spring up meet primarily in homes and rarely have more than a half dozen core people attached to them. We tend to average about eight people in a liturgical meeting, no matter how many people are currently attached to that group.

What is fascinating is that groups spring up and shut down as needed and these groups are almost always new mixtures of people. Pastorally, it has been an exciting challenge learning how to care for the groups that rise up and at the same time how to maintain the network of relationships that represents our real community. We learned the hard way not to push groups into existence; rather, when it seems like a new group is ready to find its way to the surface, we gather the people interested in starting this new group and we simply pray.

After a few years of trying to establish a viable Sunday service we began to realize that we should instead focus on what God was actually blessing and not worry about the rest. Sundays have never really worked for our community. Twice we have made serious attempts at running regular Sunday services, even once renting a nice big auditorium for weekly meetings. But, the heart of Freedom is in the relationships that are cultivated through the small groups, so it is on these small groups that we decided to focus. Instead of developing another place to do church, we turned our attention to making these home groups serious liturgical settings by paying careful attention to how each unique group of people worships, and adjusting the liturgy (order of worship) to fit the particular needs of that group.

Our running joke is that we never celebrate the Eucharist the same way twice; this is not entirely true, but it gives you an idea about where our values rest. Our commitment is to the community of people, not the forms of ministry. This shift in focus from forms to relationships gives us incredible freedom in the variety of ways our groups are able to express themselves.

Discovering Mission as a Community

Our evangelical heritage gives us a real passion to see other people encounter God. Even early on in planting Freedom we would dream and scheme about ways to connect with our friends and neighbours. Many of us had grown skeptical of the effectiveness of traditional methods of evangelism, particularly the confrontational models. While these models offer a dramatic approach to evangelism, really none of us have seen these methods produce much in the way of lasting fruit. In our experience, when you invest time, love, and energy into the lives of others, then people who experience Christ through this ministry tend to develop an unshakable commitment to living out the same good news that they experienced through our lives. The reality is that this kind of evangelism is costly (time, energy, and money); it is almost never easy.

Evangelism like this can take years and always has the real possibility of not ending in the way that you hope. But we are convinced that this is more akin to the expressed love of God: God offered Jesus in the hope that we would all embrace the gift of salvation. To describe this missional stance we have employed a slogan: "One step closer to the Father." As a community we have thrown ourselves into the messy and wonderful process of helping all the people in our lives see and commit to a better vision of God. We encourage one another to live as Christ in this world, and as a community we create space for that to happen. To facilitate and model this, our home groups are encouraged to include some sort of non-liturgical social gathering each month; these gatherings have been a major part of introducing new folks to our community.

Formation and Discipleship

People who transition into our liturgical settings find that we take the corporate role of promoting spiritual maturity seriously. As a church we actually focus more on formation than conversion. Folks who come out are invited to participate in the service regardless of where they are at in their relationship with God.[1] Despite being unabashedly liturgical, we believe that our community is a safe place for folks to jump in and encounter God.

Formation that happens in these settings includes developing a strong relationship to the Scriptures. We foster this relationship in three ways: by creating a dynamic relationship with the narratives of the Gospels, by emphasizing a teaching grounded in the Scriptures, and by fostering a corporate dialogue in which we participate with the Scriptures. This scriptural formation happens mainly through our liturgical settings which follow two distinct forms. The first form is a traditional Vineyard formula consisting of three crescendos: worship in song, teaching, and praying for each other. The teaching in this form is almost always structured around that day's lectional Gospel reading. The format of teaching can vary from a discussion to a structured sermon, but the small setting allows even the most structured sermon to become interactive.

The second form our liturgy takes is Eucharistic. This form rarely ever includes a sermon, but it always includes the public reading of Scriptures. To proclaim Scripture aloud has been a novel idea for us; it allows us to simply receive the words as they are.[2] Reading in this way places the words of Scripture into the context of a celebration oriented toward the encounter of God; we encounter Christ through the words as opposed to encountering a teaching. In addition we have borrowed an ancient practice of having baptismal candidates read the entire Gospel of Mark with their sponsor on the night before their baptism. For many, even for sponsors who have been Christians for years already, this is often the first time they have read an entire Gospel from beginning to end in one sitting.

Our commitment to reading the Scriptures allows the Word of God to live and breathe in our midst more so than we had previously experienced through messages that simply hop through the epistles. What continues to amaze us is the biblical literacy of our adherents; they are not just familiar with verses but they know the story and they are not afraid to point out when a teacher takes a verse out of context. Obviously, this changes the way we approach teaching from the Scriptures. Rarely will you hear a teacher at Freedom building cases for ideas with a collection of disconnected verses. We train and encourage those who teach and lead discussions to stay close to the lectional readings of the day and to wrestle with them for a word that speaks to our group. Lectional readings are great for ensuring that our home groups cover a variety of important subjects every year and connect our liturgy to a rich historical Church calendar.

We have also introduced into the times of discussion an exercise that develops a dialectic relationship with the Scriptures. Real dialogue moves in two directions. Much of our previous experience in the church has consisted only of starting with the Scriptures and trying to distill a message. The dialectic exercise works in both directions. We start by discussing our lived experience; we talk about our frustrations and fears, our needs and desires. We drill deep into these issues, asking why and how we can live in a world of stark injustice and intense suffering. Then we take our concerns to the Scriptures, particularly the Gospel reading for that day. We ask what that reading says to our situation and also what that situation says to the reading. Through this type of teaching we learn together how to enter into a dialogue with the Scriptures, trusting that in the Scriptures we encounter the God who meets us in the midst of real life.[3]

When we finally stopped trying to do all the things that are expected of a traditional church, specifically the things that were not working for our community, life actually became simpler. In this newfound simplicity we are suddenly able to focus on relationships in a more open and relaxed way. Discipleship became something that happened not through a deliberate program, but rather through being present in each others' lives. From our experience of developing relationship- focused community we are better able to recognize the real discipleship needs in our community and to respond specifically to those needs. In fact, some of the workshops we developed to disciple our people have so impacted us that we also delivered them to other congregations.

Taking Risks to be Faithful to the Gospel

Our strong relationship with the Word of God opens up our social conscience. We realize that far from teaching an escapist triumphalism, the Scriptures reveal the incarnational God who enters into the suffering of humanity in order to be a Word of hope. This hope speaks of the transformation of all that has been ravaged by sin, whether that sin be relational, societal or even political. Quite a few of us are no longer able to turn a blind eye to the rape of our planet any more than we can suffer the rape of a fellow human being.[4] We are willing to take risks on doing what we believe to be right. We encourage one another to consider the political implications of the gospel.

We also take risks to reach those we see as virtually abandoned by the conservative evangelical Church. Our conviction is that it is almost impossible to significantly share Christ with people you are not willing to have as part of your life. For example, at Freedom, a number of us have made a point of being an active presence at local gaming conventions.[5] Over the years we have built strong relationships with various gamers in our city which gives us incredible opportunities to be Christ in their lives. We are not outsiders pretending to be insiders; many of us are actually avid gamers ourselves. What we discovered is that there is a deep longing for life companions who are spiritually mature, wise and loving. We refuse to abandon to the world people in need; we have made a point of opening up our lives to meet folks where they are at.[6]

We use our strengths of community building as a way of being a blessing to the world. As a church, we encourage our people to form and join affinity groups based on areas that already interest them. These groups are not an official part of our church, but as a church we pray into the relationships from which these groups spring up. Most of the affinity groups that have emerged among our adherents are built around games and movies. It is important for us to make the distinction that these are not deliberate evangelistic outreaches, but opportunities to build real relationships and find places to show the love of Christ to our friends and neighbours. As we build these relationships, it is important not to be covert about our faith. In these relationships we are always on the look-out for the natural ways to live our faith before these people, many of whom have never encountered non-judgmental Christians who were open about their faith.

Affinity groups not only provide a natural network, they also yield an opportunity to step out in faith. Within these affinity groups it is important for us to model a life of faith as a natural part of our lives. By far, one of the most exciting ways this is accomplished is through prayer. We like to jump at opportunities to pray for the needs that arise in all of our spheres of influence. Letting a family know that your whole church is praying for their specific need is always an incredible witness. We focus on expressing God's love as a primary motivation for prayer, but we have also found that God is near to all who pray. God often shows up in the lives of the folks around us, and it is only natural that they turn to the safe people of faith when this happens.

God's Heart for the World

In all of our spheres of influence we find people who are living through the messiness of life. One of the great advantages of practicing what we call long-haul evangelism is that people get to see us, warts and all. They realize that being a Christian is not a great panacea that solves every problem; on the contrary, our lives are filled with just as much trouble as everyone else's (John 16:33). But, seeing how we love and accept each other, even in the midst of some horrible situations, is one of the most powerful witnesses we can offer. It is not uncommon for our adherents to express gratitude for the unconditional acceptance they experience from our people; acceptance that draws them into their own relationships with God.

Love in our community is expressed powerfully through our ability to care for each other in times of financial need. A huge advantage of not having the overhead of a building is the ability to respond freely to needs that arise both inside and outside of our congregation. We have tried to model generosity and it has become contagious. I have personally witnessed amazing and even sacrificial generosity being practiced by our people.[7]

Seeing love expressed in a community that cares deeply for each other draws people from the affinity groups into our official church activities. Most often they will transition to home group games or movie nights. Sometimes they will come out to a concert or a party. And some of those will continue to be drawn into our liturgical settings and eventually into the waters of baptism.

Worship as Witness

I have already mentioned that our home groups are unabashedly liturgical. It is always interesting to see new people come into a home group. A few years back a gentleman showed up for our Ash Wednesday celebration; his first comment was, "This had better not be Pentecostal." Clearly he had some questionable history with Christians so I simply encouraged him to grab a coffee and enjoy himself. Ash Wednesday is an important celebration for Freedom because at the time we happened to run most of our home groups on Wednesday nights. The format on Ash Wednesday is our Eucharistic service, but with a time of marking wrists with ashes using the declaration, "Turn away from sin and be faithful to the gospel." Whoever is leading also prays a personal blessing over the person who comes forward to receive the ashes. This service has been a profound part of our church life and a beautiful way to kick off Lent. Well, I could see that this visitor was a bit uncomfortable with the service; perhaps it was the lively singing. So while I was blessing people with ashes his cell phone rang. What had happened was God had answered a prayer he had made earlier. After the call he began to share this with us. What was most touching was that he then came forward, received the ashes, and encountered the love of God in a profound way.

The reason we gravitate towards a more traditional form of liturgy has a lot to do with recognizing a deep longing in the hearts of the people in our community. A number of our congregants have either a Catholic or an Anglican background. So when we began exploring what it means to be a Eucharistic community, it was only natural to look at the Roman Catholic liturgy. After a few years of experimentation we have settled on a Roman Eucharistic form which we have adapted to better fit our conservative evangelical convictions.[8] For many people in our church, the Eucharist has become the high point in our corporate worship life.

The other significant shift in our Eucharistic theology is in terms of who is invited to participate at our communion table. In keeping with our commitment to everyone being invited to participate we developed a theology of an 'open table.' Typically communion is a 'closed table' reserved for the baptized or even just for the specific membership of a particular congregation. To go to the lengths we do to include people in all aspects of our services, it no longer made sense to have an area where some people were excluded from participation, especially when the Eucharistic practice had become so central to our spirituality as a community. Our theology of an "open table" is rooted in our conviction that it is the encounter of God which transforms our lives. When we spend so much effort building places and services where our friends and neighbours can experience God it is only natural that we open up the Eucharist to them as well. As we moved toward an 'open table' we were also mindful that communion is a sacred encounter, not to be taken lightly. In deference to the sanctity of the Eucharist we open the invitation, but at the same time make it clear that no one feel coerced into participation.

Dependence on the Holy Spirit

Regardless of what forms of liturgy each home group gravitates towards, prayer is always a non-negotiable. We will not start a home group without first gathering in prayer. The crescendo of prayer is always a part of every liturgical gathering. As I mentioned already, prayer is a huge way in which we demonstrate how we care for each other. We encourage everyone to pray during that part of our service. This often can surprise new people who are not used to being invited to participate so fully in church. One summer we had a couple of Roman Catholics from Latin America join one of our home groups. After the service they came up to me and informed me that it was the priest who always prayed for the people. I just encouraged them to pray silently if that is what they are more comfortable doing. By the end of that summer I was overjoyed as one of these ladies led us in prayer at a coffee shop where we had gathered. Neither of these ladies expects the priest to do all the praying anymore.

Kingdom of God

The focus on active participation in our home groups is really how we express our theology of the Kingdom. Our Vineyard heritage has strong ties to the Kingdom theology of George Eldon Ladd.[9] This theology stresses the eschatological tension of the now and not yet of God's Kingdom; it is really what sets the Vineyard apart from other Pentecostal denominations. For Jesus, the Gospel is the good news of the Kingdom, and whenever Jesus announces the Kingdom there is always an invitation to orient our lives to what the Kingdom looks like. We see the Gospel as an invitation to work with God towards the goals of the Kingdom: peace, justice, love, hope, and faith. As a church we model active participation rather than passive observation.

We have also found that hands-on workshops are very effective in creating an anticipation of God's expressed reign. One of our most popular workshops is a focus on the prophetic dimension of faith life. We help one another understand the unique ways in which each of us receives the voice of God. What is important for us is that we all learn how to participate in the prophetic and not simply let others hear on our behalf. Because we run several exercises designed to help individuals realize that this is a natural part of the Christian experience, we find that the atmosphere in following home groups is charged with expectation. This type of equipping is the key to our eagerness to turn to prayer. We have seen many powerful examples of the in-breaking presence of God's Kingdom. We long to be a people of God's presence in this world.

Missional Authority

Pascal understood that we could only convince the mind. But when we simply live out the Gospel and not try to convince anyone, people will be convinced by the witness of our authentic lives and long for that in their own lives.[10] Our strongest evangelism comes from just being who we are. Being a church that is more concerned about building relationships than having a polished worship service has opened up doors for us that we never expected. Despite not being the traditional Vineyard we set out to plant in Ottawa, Freedom has far exceeded our expectations as to how a church can impact lives.

But being this kind of church demands a different set of sensibilities. We have to throw out the typical measures of success. Playing the numbers game actually leads some local churches to not consider us as a 'real' church. For us it has nothing to do with the numbers of people we see worshiping in the home groups. It is about the quality of our ministry to whoever comes into our spheres of influence. If we help our friends move "one step closer to the Father," then we are hugely successful. And I know for a fact that we have helped many gain a better understanding and commitment to God.

Part of the Vineyard heritage is the passion to equip and release. Over the years we have seen some amazing people come out to Freedom. Some of those people came out for just a season and then took what we gave to them to other churches and cities. We have made it a point to bless the comings and goings of all our people. It is always hard to see people go, but it is more important for us to be faithful to God. When new people show up at Freedom we pour ourselves into them as much as we can for as long as they are with us. Planting Freedom has demanded that we be flexible and allow things to be born, die, and become something new. Success for us is never maintaining, but it is about following the ebbs and flows of life as a community of the Spirit.[11]

Where do we go from here?

Throughout the journey of planting Freedom Vineyard we have had many different small groups come and go. We never know what is going to spring up next. When new small groups come to life they bring whole new groups of people ready to experience our kind of community. Because the journey is so exciting we have decided to not be in a rush. Our mentoring pastor from Sarnia, George Esser, likes to remind us that there are no emergencies in the Kingdom of God. So we are taking our time listening to the Spirit and following when and where God's Spirit leads. Only God knows what the future has for us. But if it is anything like what we have already seen, then I cannot wait.

About Frank Emanuel

Frank Emanuel is a Vineyard pastor and sessional lecturer at Saint Paul University in Ottawa. He has served in various pastoral roles since 1991. Frank's love for the Church and theology has led him into researching the political theologies that are emerging at the edges of evangelicalism. He is married and has two wonderfully creative daughters. Frank writes, reflects and blogs at freedompastor. blogspot.com and oversees a theological and pastoral writing team for the Canadian Vineyard at blog.vineyard.thoughtworks.org. In addition, Frank has published various articles on worship, liturgy, and evangelicals.

Bibliography

Barrett, Lois Y., et al. *Treasure in Clay Jars: Patterns in Missional Faithfulness.* Grand Rapids: William B. Eerdmans, 2004.

Hunter, George G. *The Celtic Way of Evangelism: How Christianity Can Reach the West - Again.* Nashville: Abingdon, 2000.

Morphew, Derek. *Breakthrough: Discovering the Kingdom.* Cape Town: Vineyard International, 1991.

Pascal, Blaise. "Pensées." No pages. Online: http://oregonstate.edu/ instruct/phl302/texts/pascal/pensees-contents.html.

1 Our model for evangelism is greatly influenced by Hunter, *The Celtic Way of Evangelism*.

2 The credit really belongs to Dr. John Gibaut who taught an excellent course on liturgy at Saint Paul University. In this course we not only explored the history of Christian liturgy, but looked specifically at how every element in the liturgy opened up the possibility to encounter Christ.

3 This is a practice adapted from Latin American base Christian communities that follow a Liberation Theology.

4 Realizing that John 3:16 (*ton kosmon*) is about the whole created order is key to the conscientisation of our congregation.

5 The main reason we focus on the convention is through the encouragement of the Christian Gamers Guild (http://www.christian-gamers-guild.org/) who make it a point to run a gamer-friendly church service at the major gaming conventions in the United States. The games we are involved with are primarily table top games like board games and pen and paper based role playing games.

6 An area which is a considerable challenge for our community is the inclusion of LGBT people. While we consider our community to be welcoming we also hold a tension of mixed understandings about human sexuality. This commitment to be welcoming has led to the loss of people on both sides of the debates primarily because of the unwillingness to live within this tension.

7 Money is also an area that proves difficult for sustaining this model of church. While we see consistent generosity in response to expressed financial needs, there is often no regular pattern of giving from which to compensate the leadership for their time and energy.

8 The form is an adaptation of Eucharistic Prayer #3 from the Roman Rite.

9 A great primer on Vineyard Kingdom Theology can be found in Morphew, *Breakthrough*.

10 Pascal, "Pensées."

11 The structure of this essay owes a huge debt to the eight "Patterns of the Missional Church" found in Barrett, *Treasure in Clay Jars*,12-14.

Chapter 6

Scaling the Church Walls: King's Bridge Community Rediscovering the Parish, Calgary
Rob Scott

Who is a part of your congregation? What groups of people make up your parish? Who belongs to your faith community? Perhaps you're tempted to answer, "The people who go to my church."

But what if the answers to those questions were turned inside-out?

Everyone I encounter is a part of my parish. Everyone I congregate with, in any setting, is my congregation. As soon as I sit down to converse with someone, they've already entered my church.

This perspective is at the heart of the King's Bridge community. This shift underscores the journey we've been on for the past fourteen years. It's a journey forward that necessitates an appropriation of the past.

When I hear someone begin a conversation about churches with the phrase, "Fifty years ago..." my eyes glaze over and I start searching for the nearest exit. I expect a glowing portrait of the Western Church's glory years to follow. I expect an indemnification of current cultural trends. I anticipate a grouchy editorial written via a very selective memory. But what you're about to read isn't going to glorify the white Anglo-Saxon Protestant past of Beaver-Cleaverdom. So bear with me through a short retrospective that begins with those infamous words.

Fifty years ago the concept of the community parish was alive and well in many areas of Canada. There were a few small churches in each urban neighbourhood. Ministers were known in the community. The sight of a man in a collar standing at a local market conversing with his neighbours was not strange. And even if you were in the minority and didn't attend church meetings, you knew where to go when you had spiritual questions. The church was an identifiable part of the community.

Of course there were all sorts of walls and barriers in this period as well. The sight of a woman in a collar would be shocking. The site of an Aboriginal, Asian, African or South American in a collar would be novel. If a Catholic visited a Baptist church on a Sunday morning it would be a tale of political intrigue. And if you wore a turban or a burka in public in late October, odds are you were heading to a Halloween party rather than a temple or mosque.

One of the great developments of our current era is the disintegration of cultural homogeneity. But the era of post-Christendom in which we now live has also melted away the reality of the church as a vital part of the community at large.

When I was in my mid-twenties, shortly after I was ordained, I conducted a funeral. I rarely wore a black suit, let alone a black shirt and clerical collar, but it was appropriate in this context for me to put on my uniform, so I did. Afterward, forgetting my costume, I made a quick stop at the grocery store. I paid for my items, turned to leave, and the man who'd bagged my groceries said to me, "Can I help you carry these to your car, Father?" I was taken aback. I wanted Luke Skywalker to pop up from behind the counter and yell, "You're not my father!" We just don't live in the era of the community priest anymore. But maybe we should. Maybe it's time for a covert operation. Maybe priests, pastors, congregants, deacons, blue-haired church ladies, sunny-faced Sunday School kids, upstanding board members, and slumbering bored members need to re-enter the community outside the church walls. Uncostumed, without recognition, position or authority, Christians can become a vital part of the community once again. This premise has piloted the King's Bridge community through several experiments and incarnations.

When King's Bridge began, our program structure defied the time-space continuum: It was the late '90s and we conducted Sunday services, child and youth ministry in a little white church building, surrounded by little white houses, attended mostly by little white people. Take away the TV screens in the sanctuary, and the rock-influenced music in the service, and you'd find yourself transported to 1952. The idea of the community parish was alive and well in our hearts and hopes. It was D.O.A. in our programs and priorities. Time travel wasn't a viable means of community connection. Almost no one outside of the Christian subculture was looking to churches as a point of connection.

So we began re-thinking. We looked at Acts 17:19 and asked ourselves, "Where is the Areopagus today?"

In the '50s and '60s the church was a community hub. Where are the community hubs today? Where do people connect beyond pre-established family, friendship and workplace relationships? What is the catalyst for these new connections? What is the core action involved in forming new bonds, new opportunities to share ideas, opinions and faith? And how do people begin to relate to each other across cultural and ideological divides?

Our search for community hubs initially brought us to cafés, pubs and university campuses.

Our search for the conduit for connection caused us to see the importance of conversation.

So we began searching for opportunities to relocate the life of our community from the little white church to campuses, pubs and cafés. We stopped trying to build services, songs and sermons, and started building conversations.

We began looking for a home base from which to radiate these new efforts. For a year we pursued a new building of our own. The idea was to launch a storefront café with a small church sanctuary in a back room. We put every penny on the table, including my full salary. We turned every eyeball in our congregation in the direction of leasable storefront spaces. We came very close to moving on a property before feeling that something was wrong. There was an indefinable sense of moving in the right direction, tainted by the wrong motives.

After much introspection, discussion, and missed opportunity we found a critical error in the core of our search. We were looking for a safe space. We were trying to rejuvenate the little white church idea by installing couches and coffee machines. We wanted to fabricate our own community hub rather than enter the post-Christian community hubs that already existed. We had control issues, and we lacked courage.

Redirected by this revelation, I began approaching owners of small, independent cafés near the University of Calgary. I pitched a program that included a weekly live music performance, and a discussion-starting short presentation. The café owners assumed we wanted to rent out their venue and use it for our program. They expected a private gathering that booked out their public space. It took some explanation on my part to convince them that we just wanted them to staff and run the café in the same manner they did every other day. We wanted the doors open. We wanted people to drop in. The band didn't mind if they came and went in the middle of the music. I didn't mind if they walked in or out in the middle of my presentation.

When we came to an agreement with a little café named the Double Mo, "come and go" is exactly what people did. I usually began by talking about a pop culture, political or social phenomenon. I then explored spiritual themes underlying this phenomenon. At the point I mentioned Jesus, I often witnessed a mini-exodus from the café. But others stayed and engaged the topic. Still more popped in after the music and message was done, diving into the conversations that had already begun.

Our band slowly replaced rock-infused Christian songs with spirit-infused secular songs. And their listeners began to hear Christian themes in the music they already loved and listened to on the radio.

I slowly replaced my pop-culture, three-point sermon model with a pop-culture three-question conversation catalyst. Disseminating religious answers from the stage wouldn't cut it in our community's new context but stirring spiritual questions would.

Midway through the first year in our new café home, I discovered something hidden within myself; something that I hadn't seen clearly during my little white church years. It was a lingering doubt that had been there for years, but was well concealed. Throughout my early years of ministry I'd paid lip service to the idea of the Holy Spirit at work in the lives of "seekers." I'd tell people about times that I saw evidence of Christ revealing his presence to those outside of the church culture. I would say that I believed Jesus pursued people, wooed them, called them, and sometimes allowed Christians to be nearby as he was doing this. But in a dark broken place within myself I wasn't sure this was true. And it showed in everything I did. I just hadn't seen it.

How did it show? Years earlier, I'd been involved in a variety of evangelistic outreaches. I always made sure the keyboard was pumping out heart-tugging chords as I built towards the altar call. Throughout my life I'd engaged in many discussions about faith with those who had different beliefs. I always attempted to fortify and forward what seemed to me to be intellectually sound apologetics. The brokenness was a subtle reliance on myself rather than Christ. I felt that it was up to me to introduce people to Jesus. I carried this burden as if God wasn't already active in other people's lives. It was up to me to make the connection. I was attempting to manipulate people toward faith.

Venturing out into a context where I couldn't as easily influence people's emotions and ideas was necessary in order for me to see that Jesus is alive and active in the world at large, with or without me. I needn't be burdened with the mandate of enticing people to follow him. I could however, follow him as he moved through the markets, meetings and menageries of our world and demonstrated his presence to those who had not yet turned their attention to him. I could enter the conversations he had already begun.

One evening at the Double Mo, I began talking with a new employee behind the counter before having to leave the conversation to jump up on the stage for the evening's presentation. During the presentation I spoke of my faith. I had been outed. As I re-entered the earlier conversation, the young man repositioned himself into a "talking to a Christian" mode. He quite brashly, and outside of the context of our discussion, declared that he was an atheist. I asked him how he'd found himself in this position. He fumbled around for a while and eventually told me that when he was a teenager, his family had attended church regularly. It had been a liberal mainline denominational congregation. He told me that he once approached the minister with questions of faith. One of the questions was, "What's the point of attending church?" He was told the purpose of the church was to allow people to come together to be comforted. They could gather together and have their worldview affirmed and feel safe from the struggles of life. He told me that in his experience this comfort was a false-panacea and he had too many questions and ideas to tolerate church anymore.

I told him that I shared some of his feelings. I felt the church should agitate as much as it comforts. It should be asking as many questions as it's answering. It should stir things up. He came alive at this idea. He said he'd definitely attend a church like that. For the next couple of months, he stood behind the counter with new questions churning inside him. On occasion, he joined me for a beer after work, and our conversation continued. And as far as I know, he never realized that he was at church the whole time. He never acknowledged that he'd found himself in our parish. Or perhaps our parish had found itself in him.

Our time at the Double Mo also accelerated our activities in social justice causes. We had worked on projects dealing with HIV/AIDS for some time. And then one evening the pandemic became much more personal.

A young South African couple was in town for several speaking engagements. On Sunday evening they would be speaking at King's Bridge's café gathering. Throughout the week leading up to this, my wife and I visited with them, introduced them to downhill skiing, and grew to really enjoy their company. They were a lot like us. They had experienced the love of Christ. They wrestled with the culture of mainstream Christianity. They were enjoying the early years of their marriage. But unlike us, they were both HIV positive. He in fact, had developed a full expression of AIDS and had nearly died before being accepted for a research trial of anti-retroviral drugs.

The café was packed on the evening they spoke. They shared simply from their experience. They shared insightfully about the situation in South Africa. They shared their faith. They shared themselves.

When they finished, I stepped up onto the stage and found myself staring into a room full of teary eyes. I didn't know what to say. And so I did something I never thought I'd do corporately in the café. I invited those gathered to join me in prayer. Atheists, Muslims, Christians and the religiously undeclared joined together in those few moments, because God had walked through the room and brushed up against us. God had revealed himself through this young couple.

That evening changed King's Bridge. One of our members went to work with children with HIV/AIDS in Romania. Another stepped into an ongoing role as an emissary of our community in Africa. For several years she worked in South Africa and Uganda with adults and children struggling with HIV/AIDS, eventually falling in love and marrying a wonderful Ugandan man who has become a member-at-a-distance of our community.

When we climbed over the little white church walls and adopted the community at large as our congregation, social justice issues ceased to be distant causes. They became practical realities. Since our exodus from the insular, mainstream church model we have always had members of our community who live on the street, members who struggle with mental illness, members pushed to the fringes of society. These situations aren't political issues, they're family struggles for our community.

After a year, The Double Mo closed its doors; another victim of the current love-affair with the MegaMcStarbucks juggernaut. We were only given six days' notice of the closure. Six days until our next event. Six days to see if God had any creative energy he wanted to pour into our void. In those six days, we were invited to move to another café, a shop named Soma. We didn't need to knock on office doors or make a pitch to owners or try to sell ourselves. Amrit, a Hindu woman and Darim, her Sikh husband, owned Soma. After we relocated to their venue, they attended almost every one of our events. They even brought their children. And while I had many vital conversations with others during our time at Soma, the deepest conversations about Christ were with them. Family considerations caused them to sell the café after we had spent a year there. When I said goodbye to them, I told Darim something very personal, not knowing how he would respond or whether I might even offend him. I told him that when I envisioned

God the Father in my mind, it was Darim's face I saw. His response was a teary-eyed embrace.

During our time at Soma we realized there was a cultural barrier in our program. While people of widely varied ages, worldviews, ethnicities and economic castes were able to find some degree of connection with the King's Bridge community, there was one group that found themselves excluded: young families. This exclusion was one of pragmatics not intent. A conversational café can't accommodate the interests and energy of small children unless it is equipped for them. The Double Mo wasn't child-friendly. Soma was child-friendly, but not well-equipped. And King's Bridge's events were neither child-friendly nor child-equipped.

As these observations rattled around in my cranium, I began to envision a business venture. It was an idea I wasn't well-positioned to pursue myself, but it seemed strange that a city of a million people hadn't yet seen it develop. There were coffee shops with small play areas for children. But what if a café was to open with a huge play area and a small quiet zone for parents to sip and chat? One day, as my wife and I drove past a vacant commercial building, we talked about how perfect it would be for this sort of venture. The next week a new tenant started renovating. A couple of month's later, they put up a sign that read "Coffee and S'cream: A Full Service Coffee Spot With Separate Area For Parent And Tot." I was floored; and excited. The next day I contacted the owners to set up a meeting to try to sell them on a new King's Bridge program. It took six months, a handful of phone calls and three meetings, but eventually they agreed to a trial program. We called it Kid's Bridge.

Kid's Bridge, much like our other café ventures, primarily attracted people from outside of the church culture. While many were sporadic in their attendance, connections deepened with several families who attended Kid's Bridge regularly. Each event was a combination of playtime for the children and discussion time for the parents. The subject matter of our discussions was usually practical and parenting-oriented. Spiritual themes were introduced as a handful of parents and I simply shared our experiences and perspectives.

One evening, a father who regularly attended, approached me outside of the parent's discussion. It was clear something was on his mind. As we began to talk, he shared that he felt he had a role in nurturing his children's faith. He had Catholic roots, but hadn't attended church in many years. He wasn't sure what he believed himself, and now he found himself responsible for two little people full of questions. The weight of his struggle was apparent. This was a difficulty that he hadn't articulated to anyone before. When spiritual and identity issues collide, people sometimes find themselves with no one to talk to. Paralyzed and guilt-ridden, they feel that God is an adversary rather than an ally. I suggested that there were several simple exploratory steps he could begin to take both for himself and his children's questions. As the conversation progressed I could see the weight lifting from his face. Near the end of the evening it became clear that he had begun to explore the idea that God could be an intimate partner in parenting, rather than a distant judge.

During the same year we began the Kid's Bridge program, Darim and Amrit, the Soma owners, experienced a family situation that compelled them to sell the café. They asked the new owner to continue to host our gathering and he agreed to do so, saying that he would give us at least a month's notice if he changed plans. The day he gained possession of the café, he reneged on his promise and told us we would no longer be able to meet at Soma. This time we found ourselves with only three days' notice. Three days until our next event. Three days that would catch me off-guard by challenging and changing the bigotry I hadn't realized lay within me.

When we launched into café-based ministry, we intentionally sought out secular locations. On occasion I would say to churchaphobic acquaintances, "Why don't you come to church and I'll buy you a beer." The secular, licensed locations we gathered in went a long way toward dissipating the Christian stereotypes that kept people from connecting. Shortly after we began pursuing our first café location, a very large church in Calgary started a café of its own. It was called The House Coffee Sanctuary. To my jaded eyes, it seemed like a hangout for the church's youth and young adult groups, rather than an open community connection point. When it opened, Christian music populated its sound system, local affluent condo-dwellers seemed more welcome than local homeless people, and the young people who gathered were of the suburban evangelical variety rather than the eclectic urban variety that lived near the café.

Of course, this perspective was only partly founded in reality. As a salve for my own identity and faith struggles, I had embraced a bigoted perspective toward mainstream Christianity. It was a blinder that kept me from seeing a remarkable evolution happening at the church-owned café in question.

When King's Bridge was faced with eviction from the Soma café, I desperately looked around for a café to host our next event and came up short. And then I swallowed my pride and called up the pastor/manager of The House Café. He immediately welcomed us to move our event to his venue. He had taken the reins of the café in its second year of operation, after I had already formed my opinion of the place.

Under his management, the evangelical majority had declined, and the indigenous urbanites of the area had been embraced. Several homeless people had found connection through the café and received assistance in getting off the street and dealing with other issues. A new, open, conversational atmosphere had emerged—an atmosphere that embraced the diversity of perspectives found in the culture-at-large. The programs at the café, which had initially been run by its mother church, had given way to gatherings run by a variety of grassroots community and faith organizations. The House had been transformed from a mainstream church outpost to a true community hub. In short, the café was now modelling much of what King's Bridge desired to become. All that prevented a meaningful partnership was my attitude.

Confronting the prejudice revealed to me through The House's transformation led me to reassess my disconnection from Church culture in general. I began to seek out other communities that were asking the same questions as King's Bridge. I discovered there were a handful of churches on similar journeys. Moreover, I discovered that there were a handful of individuals within even the most stalwart evangelical circles who were moving beyond the walls of their communities. Jargon is often more polarizing than illuminating. But for better or for worse, my reconnection with other churches brought me into "the emerging church conversation," and gave me the term "missional" to describe the efforts of the King's Bridge community.

Over the years we've continued to change and stretch as we seek to connect. Our band moved into stand-alone evening gigs in the café and then in a variety of pubs. I dropped my spoken word presentations and moved out into the neighbourhood with a video camera. I'd ask questions of people on the street and then edit the answers into a conversation-starting film played at The House. These on-the-street interviews frequently drew people into the café to see their interview, and sometimes drew them into a deeper community connection. And even as they were drawn in, we were drawn out: Out to conversations in the pot-smoke-laced, open courtyard two blocks away from the café; Out to the front of the tattoo parlour across the street; Out to the window shoppers around the corner; Out to the New Age bookstore down the street; Out to the park a few blocks away where we'd have weekly summer barbecues that people from around the community would come to.

In recent years, my attempts to connect with other missional church communities brought me into contact with a young man named Rohadi who was just beginning to develop a new community called Calgary Church. That group is now fully partnering with both King's Bridge and The House Coffee Sanctuary to create a new multi-nodal sort of church. Out of this partnership we've begun Sunday services where the three communities converge into one. What was once a King's Bridge exclusive small group merged with a similar group run by The House. Now that combined group meets for a weekly meal where we're joined by a number of the street kids and older homeless people in the neighbourhood. It's not a meal we serve to these members of our community, it's one we eat together. The designations of "us" and "them" have broken down under the influence of growing relationships.

The handful of personal interactions I've described here are emblematic of the connections we find ourselves making through our church community. Those who would call themselves King's Bridgers are few, but the conversations are many. We often come alongside people at the beginning of an emerging dialogue with God. Sometimes we even get to help catalyze that conversation. On rare occasions we've been able to see that catalytic process through from its initiation to the point where someone more fully enters the embrace of Christ. The moments of decision are wonderful, but it's the early part of the spiritual journey that we've gravitated towards. It's the initial life questions that compel people to pursue Christ which we find most compelling.

Fewer and fewer people in Canada have Christian roots to draw on. While the number of people initiated into the Church subculture drops, the number of people longing for connection keeps growing. It's growing inside cozy cafés and on chilly street corners, online and offline, in relationships and in solitude. The longing is drawing together a new kind of congregation, a new kind of parish, one that can't be enumerated or homogenized. This new community may seem hostile to Church culture, but it's open to Christ. It may seem uninterested in joining the church community, but it's open to the church community joining it. It may seem ephemeral, but it's captivated by the eternal. It may seem disembodied, but I believe it is the body of Christ.

About Rob Scott

Rob Scott has been the Community Director of King's Bridge (www.crossthebridge.ca) since its inception in 1999. He has ministered in a diversity of settings including small Chipewyan villages in the Northwest Territories and migrant worker camps on the Baja Peninsula. Most of his work has been among the varied communities and personalities that make up inner city Calgary. Rob is an ordained minister in the Communion of Evangelical Episcopal Churches and is a provincially registered clergy person in Alberta. He currently lives in Calgary with his wife and twin daughters.

Chapter 7

LifeBridge Community Church: Strategic Discipleship, Dartmouth
Rob Laidlaw

Our adventure started with a simple phone call to an old school buddy. I was not planning on being a church planter. I had no strategic plans to look for new work beyond my existing ministry as an associate pastor in Winnipeg. Everything was going fine, until that one phone call.

David Tonen and I went to school together in Dartmouth, Nova Scotia, from grade five through to graduation. I had left Nova Scotia to pursue Bible College and then a pastoral career; I had now been away for twenty years. David pursued a career in marketing with a brief stint in Toronto, but then returned to Nova Scotia to continue his marketing career from his seaside home, which he affectionately refers to as his "anti-Toronto."

The phone call was merely a chat between old friends reflecting on the good old days and the friends we had in common in high school. Dave had not been a Christian when we knew each other in those days. He accepted Christ into his life long after I had left. So now, with Christ as a common denominator in our lives, we discussed various old friends in Dartmouth who we would like to direct toward Jesus Christ. The problem was this: where could we encourage them to attend church to explore a relationship with Jesus? There were great churches in the area, but none in which we were overly confident were designed to embrace a person who had little or no previous church experience. The bridge between Church "culture" and the surrounding culture seemed a bit too wide. I don't mean embracing culture in a watering-down-of-spirituality sort of way, but simply being able to meet people where they were at and in terms that they would understand. The call ended with no answer, no resolution to the problem of finding a church for our friends.

Go Or Stay?

Over the next several days and weeks the question kept running through my mind, "Am I supposed to move back to Nova Scotia and design a church that would be focused on mission in the local context?" I am the type of person who keeps coming up with different project ideas with the majority simply staying as "good ideas," never becoming reality. So, when I raised the idea of us moving to Nova Scotia to start an outreach-focused church to my wife Julie, she politely smiled and humoured me, trusting that the phase would soon pass, along with many of my other ideas. Julie had grown up in Manitoba her whole life. All her friends and family were there. She had been at the church for 18 years and had many deep relationships. The thought of moving across the country to start a church plant on the east coast was nowhere on her radar.

It soon became evident that moving to Nova Scotia was not part of God's plan as various events in Winnipeg necessitated our staying there…at least for the moment. If there was no emotional buy-in by my wife, then it wasn't even an option to consider. However, one year later, David Tonen and I replayed an identical conversation about needing a church for our friends to attend. This time God had prepared Julie's heart to be on the same page as my own (God just knew she needed a year's advance notice to adjust to the plan). This time Julie was the one saying we needed to go to Nova Scotia to start a church plant. We started to make plans.

I'm a firm believer in the unity of the Spirit. It was important to me that if God was behind this, he would provide affirmation not just from my wife, but from our denomination, present church board, church family and even our young children. All of the above gave us their blessing and affirmation and as a result, six months later we were living in Nova Scotia.

Denomination or No Denomination?

One challenge we faced was the question of whether or not to start an independent work or come under the umbrella of a denomination. The Baptist General Conference we were serving in at that time did not exist east of Montreal and there was some question as to whether or not they could practically be of support to a church so far away. After some discussion, we decided that going with a denomination was very critical for a variety of reasons. We knew that the "style" of church we were planning was not as familiar in the Maritimes and as such, not being under a denominational label, we would be more susceptible to being viewed as a cult. But even more so, we didn't want to be alone. We wanted to be under an umbrella of accountability. We wanted a framework of relationship with other churches for support and encouragement. We wanted to be part of a larger team.

Fortunately, the Baptist General Conference embraced the idea, adjusted their national perspective, and blessed us with the mandate to plant a church in Nova Scotia under their umbrella. It was a huge risk for them, but they took that leap of faith and encouraged us in so many ways. What a huge blessing it has been to belong to a larger network.

We're Here, Now What?

Now that we were in Nova Scotia the challenge of starting the church began. David's wife, Shelly, would ask, "So how do we get from being a group of four adults and two young children to a fully functioning church?" Never having been involved with a church plant, my response was a confidence-inspiring, "I have no idea." I truly didn't, but I trusted that God had a plan.

We held two preview services encouraging Christians and non-Christians to come out and give us feedback on our service style. Since we unashamedly asked churches to help with music, drama, child care, special music, etc., on some Sundays we had over six different churches from five different denominations helping, all at the same time. The partnership of these churches in the broader Kingdom was so invaluable and encouraging to us. By the time we hit our Easter launch service we had a consistent congregation of about forty people. Close to half of these were people not previously attending any church. Our desire was, and still is, that at least twenty to thirty percent of our Sunday morning congregation be non-Christians.

Defining Our Mission

In trying to figure out what would be the focus or overall mission of the church, we honed in on the question of our purpose in life. Why are we here? We noticed throughout Scripture that God consistently called us to relationship with him and then to invite others to that relationship. So we started out saying LifeBridge's purpose was to connect people to God and help them discover and live out his purposes for their lives. We defined these purposes by saying God created us to: 1) Be in **relationship** with him and his family, and, 2) **Represent** his love and truth in this world. We're all about R&R. We even structured our church organizationally around these two purposes.

As we planned the church we knew we could abandon any manmade church traditions in the way we styled our services, but it is amazing how much we still confined ourselves to what we knew. This became evident to me when after just a few services our worship leader announced he did not feel he was supposed to continue. We had been coming to the same conclusion, but his departure left us with a music void – a complete music void. We had no other musicians or vocalists. My reaction was, "We have to have music; every church has music." God gently spoke thoughts to my mind, "No, you don't." Obviously God needed a bit of correcting and so I responded with, "Yes, we do. You can't have church without music. No one would come." With a little more force and clarity, God then reminded me that Jesus never had a worship band, yet he built his Church. The Apostle Paul never had a worship band, but he planted churches all over Asia Minor. God was simply communicating that our mission was to preach the gospel to change lives. Even without music we could still continue with our mission, and we did.

I still led one song each week with guitar, just to keep the concept of singing alive. But that was something we more endured than enjoyed. Keep in mind, when half our congregation was non-churched, didn't know the songs and were not used to singing, "worship" was painful and in some ways an actual barrier to their comfort level. But now, with virtually no music, the question remained as to how we were going to fill our time.

We chose to spend more time developing other creative ways of getting the point of the message across to the people. Every week we spent at least thirty minutes on using the arts and object lessons to teach, in addition to the message. Over the following year, the creative energy to keep coming up with these ideas started to wear me down and cause creative burnout. Fortunately, others stepped up to form a Creative Team so that the weight did not rest solely on my shoulders. Even today this team continues to shape the design and creativity of all of our services. The result is that people have been very engaged and the message of the day hits home on many different levels.

We're Not Here For You

"We're not here for you" was a phrase we became very comfortable saying. We effectively turned many Christians away from our church with those few little words. We knew that church plants often attract disgruntled Christians from other churches who may have a tendency to come with their personal expectations. We knew, in the early days of starting a church, that this type of perspective could be a cancer that could divide a church and sway it off its mission. It's not that we didn't want other believers to come and help, it's just that we wanted them to come with a sacrificial, missional mindset. None of us who started the church did so with a sense of how it would meet our personal needs. We did it to meet the spiritual needs of others.

The reactions to the "we're-not-here-for-you" speech were varied. Some were offended and we never saw them again. Others were compelled by our focused mission and found it expressed the longing of their heart to see others reached for Christ. Those who stayed became family and were committed to seeing the church move forward, not for their personal preferences, but for its effectiveness for Jesus. Behind the scenes, every day, we fervently prayed, "God, bring the people who you are drawing to yourself. Bring the people you want here to grow your Kingdom. Keep away anyone who would bring division and who would cause us to move away from our mission." God seriously answered those prayers.

Leadership Crises

I still don't know where all the people came from, but God kept bringing people who were searching to know him. This was wonderful, but it also started to create a deep concern for us. We were running out of spiritually mature leaders who could continue to meet the needs of a growing church. We knew we needed leaders quickly or we would implode as a church plant. The problem was that you can't create leaders quickly; it takes time, a long time. However, we knew we needed to start the process of developing spiritually mature people who could rise into leadership positions soon. The only question was, "How?"

We realized Jesus accomplished this task within three years. He took a group of men who started out as skeptics and within three years built into their lives in such a way that he was then able to leave, return to heaven, and entrust the future of his Church into their hands (with the Holy Spirit's help). Wow! Could we do the same? Could we bring skeptics into our church and build into their lives in such a way that in a few short years they could be unleashed with confidence, to assume responsibility for the spiritual growth of others and potentially plant other churches? It dawned on us that this understanding of discipleship was to be the main focus and goal of everything we do at LifeBridge. Discipleship was no longer a ministry of the church; it was the ministry of the church.

We started to map out what we felt we would need to build into people's lives for us to have that degree of confidence in sending them out as spiritual leaders. We quickly realized we couldn't pull it off in three years as Jesus did, but we could cover the basics in five years. We were not aware of any existing small group curriculum that was designed to accomplish our specific goals. So we started to write … and write….and we still continue to write. The church saw this as such a priority that they commissioned me to take blocks of time off throughout the year that I would dedicate solely to writing the curriculum. They experienced the initial benefits and they longed to move forward in the discipleship process. We also agreed to offer any material we created for the Kingdom, free of charge, to any other church that would like to use it. We have several churches now utilizing this discipleship curriculum.

Since we needed to keep adding several new groups each year, it necessitated that we continually develop small group leaders who could teach the curriculum to others. Every small group then had a main teacher, an apprentice teacher, a shepherd and possibly an apprentice shepherd. Three to four small group leaders in every group created a huge resource drain on other areas of ministry, but this training was so essential to our core ministry and goal of the church that we were willing to pay that cost.

Local Impact

We rebelled against the idea that the church needs to be more involved in the community. That concept didn't even make sense to us. The church is already thoroughly enmeshed in the community. Wherever a person from our church walks, the church is there, represented through them. For us, the solution to local impact was not in creating a need-based mission outreach program, but simply equipping our people to be Salt, Ambassadors, Image and Light within all the realms of influence that God had placed them. We talk about how we need to SAIL into our various communities. We are committed to the idea that God has placed every believer in places where he wants his love and truth represented. If we could get our people simply doing that, then there would be no need for an outreach program. That is not to say we won't have small groups of people doing things within our community. It is saying that our primary focus of outreach would be through every believer in their everyday life.

It takes people a while to get used to the idea that we don't expect them to necessarily stay at our church forever. Jesus did not spend all that time training his disciples so that they would stay together as one little cozy group. They were equipped to go. Our perspective has been that we want people to be so well equipped that a good number of them will leave to plant another church or go on missions. We are working toward that goal. The fifth year of our discipleship curriculum will focus the entire year on these various mission goals with the hope that we will then continuously prepare people to leave. Instead of keeping our most well-trained people and making "our" little church stronger, we want to send them out to build God's Kingdom elsewhere.

Third World Poverty

As a young church plant we wanted to set the concept of missions deeply within our DNA. With a congregation of only about forty people, some felt it was too soon to take on a significant missions project, but God was stirring the passion and we needed to act. A missions focus on poverty was the easiest to get off the ground, and so that's where we started. We chose to partner with Compassion in Honduras as a foot-in-the-door approach to the country. We had people from our church sponsor children from two Compassion projects only five kilometres apart. As a very small church plant we were excited to see over twenty young children sponsored. But this was only to be the beginning as God then opened doors to other ministries in the area. A multi-ministry impact was always our goal.

How can we as a church focus so much on ourselves when others have never yet heard of Jesus or have no Bible in their own language? It frustrates me that we have not yet ventured into this aspect of our mission mandate, but it is not off the radar. Someone once said there is one unreached people group for every 500 churches. I don't know about the reliability of those figures, but the concept sure hit home. We need to be one of those 500 churches that chooses to do something. Jesus said it would even speed up his return. I'm all for that.

Be Careful What You Ask For

In the first year during one of our small group bible studies, we noted that Jesus' ministry was focused around preaching the Kingdom, healing and casting out evil spirits. We also noted that when he sent out the twelve and the seventy on their mission experiences, they too incorporated these same three areas of impact. As a typical Baptist church, we understood the basics of preaching the Kingdom, but we were really foggy on the healing and spiritual warfare side of things. So we naively prayed that if God wanted us to be involved in these two other areas of ministry, he would need to put us on a learning curve. That proved to be a very dangerous prayer to pray.

God started sending us people who had blatant demonic issues. Having had no previous experiences with spiritual warfare (or at least not that we had identified as spiritual warfare) of this nature, our learning curve definitely skyrocketed. After personal study, reading dozens of books and even calling authors to talk with them, we started making headway and helping people experience freedom. You need to understand, we were not looking for this, but because we declared ourselves open to dealing with it, God sent people our way whom he wanted to set free. Barely a week goes by when we are not dealing with this nature of ministry. In hindsight, it only makes sense. The very spirits Jesus dealt with are still here today. We have learned how this is really part of the discipleship process and our people need to be competently equipped to deal with it when it arises.

Back To the Main Point

As the church grew up over the 100 mark in attendance, we noticed it was getting increasingly difficult to maintain the same sense of vision. There was some discussion when we set a policy that any Partner (our version of church membership) had to be part of the discipleship process. To us, this only made sense. If our church was to be all about discipleship, then anyone who was going to help the church move forward had to be personally committed to being discipled. The real discussion came when we also stated that anyone who wanted to continue to be discipled after year three in the discipleship process needed to be a Partner. How could we cut people off from learning just because they didn't want to officially join our church? How could we say no to someone who wanted to keep on learning?

These were excellent questions and worthy of discussion. The answer for us came from a better understanding of our mission which forced us to clarify our mission. The goal of our church was not simply to spiritually educate people. We were here to introduce people to Jesus Christ, equip them, and then send them out into the world. The bottom line was we wanted to create a community where everyone grew to the point of assuming responsibility for the spiritual growth of others.

Can you imagine when Jesus sent the twelve into nearby towns, how he would have responded if one of the disciples said, "I'm not really interested in assuming spiritual responsibility for others. I just want to hang around you and listen to you teach?" How long would that discipleship process have continued? Jesus was on a mission to create leaders and leaders had to start assuming responsibility for the mission.

If we are here to create a people who will go into the world assuming responsibility for the spiritual growth of others, then it only made sense that that should start at the very place they were being equipped. Keep in mind that church partnership for us simply states, "I want to be part of the team that fulfills the church mission. I want to assume responsibility, along with others, to see the church be effective." That's it. We felt that if after three years of discipleship someone was not able to assume some degree of responsibility for their own church family, then there was a disconnect in their understanding of the goal of discipleship. They could still rotate through the first three years of Growth Groups, but we wanted them to come to a point of conviction about their role in the Kingdom, and to step up and take ownership of the mission. Some people left our church.

We decided we were not interested in collecting people. We were interested in creating world-changers. We were interested in developing a community of people who could effectively make disciples wherever they went in this world.

What's exciting is that we are into year four of our discipleship process and are seeing people who were atheists, Buddhists, New Agers as well as bored, nominal Christians now serving as ministry leaders, teachers, shepherds and evangelists. We are now seeing our first wave of people preparing to be pastors or elders who could potentially be sent out to start new churches. What's truly exciting is that one of those high school friends David and I talked about in those early phone calls became a Christ follower in our church and is now actively involved in ministry. God is good.

I feel guilty. I've talked with other church planters who have had a difficult calling. I've been part of the conversations when people ask, "Was planting a church a challenge?" and others respond with a groaning affirmation. That has not been our story. Church planting has been a relatively easy adventure that we've enjoyed every step of the way.

I don't know why God allows some to have a challenging calling (as with Jeremiah) and others an easier one. Personally, I think God knew I was a wimp who needed an easy calling. But this is simply to say, I have loved every step of being a part of this wonderful experience. May God continue to raise up people with courage to step out in faith to see God's Kingdom grow!

About Rob Laidlaw

Rob Laidlaw is currently the lead pastor of LifeBridge Community Church in Dartmouth, Nova Scotia. His growing passion for outreach and discipleship led him to take a risky step of faith to start a church plant in his hometown. Beginning with four adults and two young children, the church has grown over seven years to approximately 130 people, most of whom were not previously attending any church. Rob has been writing discipleship curricula, which he makes available free of charge to other churches through his ministry and website www.StrategicDiscipleship.com.

Chapter 8

Little Flowers Community: A Three-Fold Cord, Winnipeg
Jamie Arpin-Ricci

For the past four years, I have had the wonderful and challenging privilege to serve as the pastor of Little Flowers Community, a small inner city church several of us planted after nearly a decade of life and ministry in Winnipeg's West End. Little Flowers (as the name alone might suggest) is not a typical church plant. Reflective of our neighbourhood, some of our members live with mental illness, struggle with poverty, and often feel alienated by Christians, being no more than the object of mission and charity. For those familiar with the pop culture, I have affectionately referred to our community as the "Island of Misfit Toys" in the Church world. Perhaps one of the most interesting aspects of Little Flowers Community is that no one had intended to plant a church in the first place.

How did such a strange little community come into being? What journey led to such an unexpected destination? While there are many factors involved in our development as a community, I wanted to focus on one particular dynamic that significantly shaped me as a church planter and pastor and thus, shaped our community. In order to do that, we need to back up and see the big picture.

A Mosaic Identity

Like many Canadians, I grew up feeling like my identity was rooted in a multitude of sources. Living in a border town in northwestern Ontario, circumstances allowed that I be born in Minnesota, providing me with dual citizenship (which I maintain to this day). My father's family was Italian, coming to Canada via Britain, whereas my mother's family was proudly French Canadian (which later led me to adopt my mother's maiden name into my surname alongside my father's). Our family attended a small evangelical church, but I attended a largely Mennonite Christian school, went to a Pentecostal youth group and occasionally attended Mass at the Roman Catholic church with my grandmother.

After graduating from high school, unsure of what I would do next, a friend convinced me to join him in a five-month discipleship and missions program with the evangelical missions organization Youth With A Mission (YWAM). I never left, and still serve as the co-director of YWAM Urban Ministries Winnipeg. While predominantly evangelical (with holiness and charismatic influences), YWAM drew participants from not only a broad spectrum of the Christian tradition, but also from nations and cultures the world over. Even in Canada, I had the gift of being one of only a few white people living in a missions community largely made up of Pacific island nationalities and Koreans. Again, this multiplicity of overlapping identities and my participation in all of them were critical to my formation, culturally and spiritually.[1]

More than three decades later, as I look back on my life, I have begun to see how important those experiences were in shaping not only the person I have become, but the nature of community and ministry I have been inspired to help form. Some might caution against the dangers of pluralism, with such uncritical diversity leaving me exposed to compromise and moral relativism. However, such concerns have largely been unfounded, and have instead allowed me to experience the diversity in humanity that I believe is reflective of our being created in the image of a Triune God.

Establishing In Context

In early 2002, my wife Kim and I moved to Winnipeg's West End to begin a new ministry centre for YWAM. We chose the West End to be our location for several reasons. In large part we felt a call to share life with people in an economically and socially struggling neighbourhood. However, the decision was made firmly when we received an invitation to move to the community by a local pastor who had a very unique ministry. Pastor Harry Lehotsky[2] was the fiery leader of New Life Ministries, a North American Baptist church in the neighbourhood. Shaped significantly by the writings of Walter Rauschenbusch (a key figure in the social gospel movement) and John M. Perkins (an African- American civil rights activist), Harry was as much prophet as pastor. Inspired by his no-nonsense, rough-around-the-edges commitment to the neighbourhood, we accepted the invitation. His only provision to helping us get established was that we located in the West End. We gladly agreed.

Harry Lehotsky and other members of New Life Ministries became critical to our development as a ministry. Not only did they provide housing for us and our team in affordable apartments that the church owned, they eventually sold us an old gang house that their Lazarus Housing ministry had restored. To this day it remains our home, community house and ministry centre. We also partnered with them in projects, providing and coordinating volunteers and participating in community events. This genuine partnership did not mean we were on the same page on every matter. In fact, rarely a week went by without Harry and me debating some aspect of politics or theology. We chose not to let those differences divide us, instead uniting around our shared commitment to a gospel of love, justice and reconciliation in our inner city community.

Harry taught us a crucial lesson: if we hoped to have any credibility among our neighbours, we'd have to stick around. In fact, he said, it would likely be more than five years before we would be seen as locals. Therefore, during those years we committed ourselves to be "students" of the neighbourhood, learning the culture, the language, the history, etc. While we were active in ministry and service, we did so primarily by partnering with established communities, organizations and churches, serving them as best we could. It was a critical time in building relationships with a multiplicity of people and groups that, again, was critical in shaping who we would become.

Third Places and the Health of Neighbourhoods

In 2007, with our place in the community having taken root, we began to look at the community, its strengths and needs, and our place in participating in the fabric of the neighbourhood. Two things immediately stood out. First, for several months of the year, Winnipeg's brutally cold winters meant that we rarely saw our neighbours (except when they made a mad dash to the bus stop or corner store). Second, we realized that in order to encounter our neighbours during those months, we needed a context in which to do so. Understandably, in inner city neighbourhoods people are very cautious about entering into a neighbour's home until relationships have been firmly established (a challenge made more difficult by our Canadian predilection for privacy).

It was at that time that I became aware of the concept of "third places." Third places represent those locations in our neighbourhoods where we have social contact with our neighbours apart from our homes (first places) and work (second places).[3] Genuine third places were rare in our community; most were either economically exclusive or unhealthy (such as gang-operated bars). To that end, we decided to try and create a third place in the neighbourhood, a space that was intentionally neutral (not a bait-and-switch outreach location), not economically driven (which meant we knew we would have to subsidize the project), lent itself to dignity (not filled with cast-off couches), celebrated regulars and location, both in geography and cultural identity. Out of that commitment The Dusty Cover used bookstore was born.

The Dusty Cover was set up in a small local storefront (again rented to us by New Life Ministries). Bookshelves lined the outer walls, with the centre space devoted to leather couches and chairs set up in a circle around coffee tables. A fresh pot of fair trade coffee was always brewing, available without cost or need of purchase. We worked hard to stock quality books and organize them to library standards, but we also knew that our main commitment was to make the space welcoming. We opened the doors and hoped it would work. And it did.

134

Before long we found ourselves building relationships with a number of regulars – people with mental illness who were unemployed (or unemployable); single mothers; elderly people who had few, if any, friends still living locally (or at all); local sex workers; and dozens of local children who, being forced to leave school property over lunch but who could also not go home, became a fixture. While we did not use the space as a ministry centre – that is, the safety and neutrality of the space demanded that we not use the context to evangelize – through building relationships, the regulars (both Christians and otherwise) knew we were Christians.

A Church Is Born

One afternoon, a few of our staff (with whom we shared life with in intentional community) were discussing having a meal together at our house later in the week. One of the regulars overheard and promptly invited himself over. Inspired by this, they began to invite people every week, which soon developed into a mid-week potluck. Suddenly, we found that we had overcome the boundary that kept our neighbours from entering our home.

Soon, dozens of people would show up for the meal. Mid-week began to be difficult for some, so it was mutually agreed to move the meal to Sunday evenings. With that change, we began to see as many as 45 people come each week. With the greater level of intimacy that came with welcoming people into our home, our guests were more open and proactive in talking about issues of faith. While the evening was still primarily about food and hanging out, if often happened that someone would ask for advice or prayer. Eventually someone brought out a guitar and songs would be sung. The music was more likely to be selections from The Arrogant Worms than anything spiritual, but we were surprised how many requested a hymn or chorus they were familiar with from childhood. And throughout it all, the group began to develop into a true community.

At one Sunday gathering, Amy, a single mom who had been our most faithful regular, approached Kim and I and said:

"You know what? I think we are a church. Will you be our pastor?"

Others affirmed the idea. We promised them we would pray about it. We knew that such a possibility existed, but we were taken back at how quickly it had developed. After much thought, discussion and prayer, we felt that this was the direction we were meant to move. However, as directors of a YWAM ministry, we also were convinced that if we were going to lead this new church plant, we needed to partner with a denomination that both shared our core values and had the ecclesiology that our ministry lacked. Not knowing what else do to, I blogged about the need and waited to see what would happen.

Within a few days I was contacted by Norm Voth, Director of Evangelism and Service Ministries for Mennonite Church Manitoba. While Anabaptism was clearly a good fit for our ministry and developing community, it was Norm's willingness to partner in a way that affirmed both of our organizational identities that sold us. And so, in January 2009, Little Flowers Community began to meet together as a formal worshipping community. Our intentional community expressions also began to grow, adding other houses of people in the neighbourhood who shared life together.[4]

Standing With The Broken

Very early in our development as a church, our community experienced a great tragedy. One of our newest members, Andrew, struggled with an untreated mental illness. Despite the encouragement of family and friends to get help, the nature of his condition made him paranoid of doctors. In the end, Andrew took his own life publicly in front of several of us. While devastating, this loss not only solidified us as a community, but it opened our eyes to the challenges that many of our friends and neighbours wrestled with. Affordable, dignified housing was so rare, yet so needed, especially for those living with mental illness.

One day, someone asked me when Little Flowers Community would get a "real church building." Struggling as I was with the loss of Andrew and supporting our other friends in the community, I responded by saying: "If we had the means to have a building, I'd rather have an apartment building where we could not only offer affordable housing that maintains people's dignity, but also foster genuine community."

Around the same time, I heard about a church that had done something similar.[5] Inspired, I blogged this dream, thinking that it might simply inspire others to think creatively. However, once again I received a call from Norm Voth. He asked us whether, if he was able to get partners around the table to bring the needed resources, if we would be willing to live into such a vision. Stunned, we agreed. And so the Chiara House initiative was born.

Chiara House is an ongoing project in which we are renovating a derelict apartment building to provide affordable housing to our community. With a third of the suites designated for those working towards greater stability in light of their mental illness, one floor will also be designated for Christian intentional community. The building is being restored intentionally to meet the unique needs of our community. The partnership, which includes Little Flowers Community, Christian businesspeople, Mennonite Church Manitoba and Eden Health Services (a Christian mental health organization), brings together unique resources and strengths to make this vision a reality. We hope that at the printing of this book, Chiara House will have opened its doors.

The Power of Collaboration

While many aspects of our story could serve as a helpful focus for this chapter, what stands out as exceptionally important is the broad reach of our relationally based collaboration, both formal and informal/non-formal. Having launched our ministry under YWAM, we found that we had the capacity as a (so-called) "parachurch" organization to build in partnership with people, churches and organizations from a broad spectrum of places. Within the first few years we had established strong ties with Baptists, Anglicans, Vineyard, a variety of non-denominational churches, as well as strong connections with the local Union Gospel Mission and Siloam Mission (two significant Christian humanitarian ministries), Winnipeg Harvest (our city's largest food bank), and several other significant groups.

That ability to be so diversely connected resulted in the unexpected capacity to build bridges between groups within the city that did not exist before. The result has been a greater sense of relational familiarity and even partnership between groups that might not have otherwise connected. In recent years, I partnered with a local inter-cultural church pastor to form the Christian Collective, a monthly gathering of

Christians who lived and/or worshipped in the West End for the purpose of relationship, prayer, mutual support and collaboration.

This creative diversity, having shaped our own spiritual formation, resulted in an intentional commitment (and adeptness) at engaging the diversity of Christian traditions in positive ways without appropriating them. While our community is decidedly rooted in our Anabaptist identity, we celebrate that it is one of many expressions that make up the rich diversity of the Body of Christ.

Such collaboration is not without its challenges. Given the nature of our community, I choose not to receive any salary for my role as pastor, despite it being a full-time role. Because that ministry is an expression of my work with YWAM, I am able to raise missionary support through a wider net of family, friends and churches (though a significant portion of our income comes from my other bi-vocational roles). Further, while we are a part of Mennonite Church Manitoba, we are an affiliate congregation, which is different from a fully associated church. This is often confusing to potential supporters: Do you work for Little Flowers or YWAM? Do you pastor a church or just "do outreach"? Are you a Mennonite pastor or not? And with the addition of my role as director of Chiara House, that will only further the confusion, I am sure.

However, the challenges of such blurred boundaries are dwarfed by the benefits. Many times the very difficulties we experience are the source of our greatest blessings. In the formation of the Christian Collective, the other pastor (who comes from a more conservative evangelical background) and I had different ideas about "which Christians" we would invite. The tension in our differing ideas and reasoning created a problem that, in the context of our trusted relationship, led to generative conversations, vulnerability and a willingness to stretch both of our boundaries.

As Canada continues to become a post-Christendom culture, the way in which different Christian traditions, denominations and organizations relate will invariably change. While the differences between these groups are often legitimate and therefore not a problem to fix, some of the divisions that resulted in power-brokering from a position of privilege will cease to be important. To that end, not only will relational collaboration across such traditional markers be beneficial, but I believe it will become essential. Such benefits will include practical concerns such as shared resources and joint missional engagement, but the greatest benefit may be our witness before a watching world. So often Christians are viewed as divisive, competitive, back-biting hypocrites. The beauty of mutual care across traditional boundaries will invite the same testimony that was offered to the early church: "See how they love one another!"

About Jamie Arpin-Ricci

Jamie Arpin-Ricci is an urban missionary, pastor, church planter and writer living in Winnipeg's inner city West End neighbourhood. He is the author of *The Cost of Community: Jesus, St. Francis & Life in the Kingdom*. He is founding co-director of Youth With A Mission (YWAM) Urban Ministries, Winnipeg with his Australian wife Kim. He has served with YWAM in Canada since 1994, bringing him to 11 nations.

Bibliography

Arpin-Ricci, Jamie. *The Cost of Community: Jesus, St. Francis and Life in the Kingdom*. Downers Grove: IVP, 2011.

Oldenburg, Ray. *The Great Good Place: Cafes, Coffee Shops, Bookstores, Bars, Hair Salons, and Other Hangouts at the Heart of a Community*. New York: Marlowe & Company, 1999.

Sine, Tom. *The New Conspirators: Creating the Future One Mustard Seed at a Time*. Downers Grove: IVP, 2008.

1 It is important for me to note here that YWAM Canada, especially in its Western Canada region, has been exceptional and somewhat unique in the mission in its affirmation of genuine diversity, shared leadership and engaged, relational decentralization. While I am all too familiar with the many legitimate concerns about YWAM as an organization, I am also continually impressed with our regions commitment to missional integrity.

2 Sadly, Harry died from pancreatic cancer on November 11, 2006. Prior to his death, he was informed that, in light of his years of service, he had been appointed as a member of the Order of Canada, the second highest honour given to Canadian citizens.

3 For an excellent introduction to third places, see Oldenburg,*The Great Good Place*.

4 To learn more details about Little Flowers Community and our Franciscan-Anabaptist identity, see my book *The Cost of Community*.

5 This story can be found in Sine, *The New Conspirators*.

Chapter 9

Metro Community Church, Kelowna
Laurence East

She was shivering uncontrollably, so severely that at first I thought she was having a seizure. All the rules of ministry were out of the window and I was about to do the very thing I advised others never to do. From the comfort of the warm cab of my truck I could see her huddled in an alcove in one of the now forebodingly darkened and empty buildings that are common in the core of our city.

Unlike many cities, no one lives downtown in ours. Kelowna's downtown simply serves as a hub of commercial and civic activity during daylight hours, and in true Canadian fashion, by 9 o'clock the streets are virtually abandoned and the atmosphere changes. After dark, those who have had the luxury of fine dining or entertainment hastily depart to the safety of the suburban sprawl in the surrounding hills.

She began screaming, which pierced through the shadows of the alcove and the freezing air, even making its way into the warmth of my truck. Jumping out, the sharp edge of -30 degrees Celsius almost took my breath away, and I realized she was wearing a pair of skin-tight jeans and a grubby white tank top. I'd never met Julie[1] before, but I'd seen her at the local homeless shelter with Darren, her boyfriend, pimp and dealer. He was nowhere to be seen, and it was his name she had been screaming at the top of her lungs. Grabbing a blanket from my truck, I wrapped it round her and began to realize I was completely out of my depth.

Julie had had a fight with her boyfriend and was coming down off crystal meth. She hadn't slept for days, was in excruciating pain and couldn't even feel the cold, although the lack of body fat and meat on her bones meant she was going to die in the frigid conditions unless I got her to a hospital. As I huddled in the alcove with her, trying to coax her circulation into action, she began to moan for water. "I need water, I need water!!!" Her moan mutated into a shriek as I tried to coax her into my truck to warm her up. I promised her water from the first gas station we'd see.

It took fifteen precious minutes to convince her to leave with me. Julie was convinced that Darren would return, her survival co-dependency kicking in hard. She was locked in a tragic cycle of dependency; he provided a vague promise of safety from the predators around her and controlled that dependency by drip-feeding her substance addiction. The title of "boyfriend" was not exclusive, but merely convenient for him when his drug-fueled rage led to violation and abuse. Julie's desperate need to be loved kept her coming back to Darren, a need enhanced by the crystal meth in her bloodstream.

It wasn't until the short ride to the hospital emergency room that it occurred to me that I had violated all of the safety protocols and boundaries that the large, suburban mega-church where I was employed had recently published for all of its forty or so staff. As the emergency duty nurses helped Julie onto a gurney and rushed her inside, the adrenaline in my system morphed into anger and frustration.

Our community is located in a city of almost 200,000 people, but Kelowna has several dubious distinctions. British Columbia and Quebec are the least churched provinces in Canada, but Kelowna stands as an anomaly. It is known as a "Bible-belt" town, with upwards of 100 churches -- and the largest homeless population for a city its size in Canada. Over a period of 20 years, all of the churches have abandoned the downtown of the city and relocated to the suburbs.

That night, when I returned to the warmth and comfort of my own home, I sat at a blank computer screen and began to write a letter to the church. In it, I implored my church to do something, anything -- and finished my diatribe with the cry, "Where is the church?" I sent it to everyone I knew, pressed Send and slumped into bed at 3:00 in the morning. John Stott once said, "Christians have been blaming the meat (of society) for going rotten when the preserving salt has been taken out of it, and the house for getting darker when the light has been removed. It is time for Christians to recognize their responsibility to be salt and light in our society."[2]

The journey and formation of the Metro Community, a small, eclectic group of people from all walks of life, is nothing short of astonishing. Unlike many church plants, the ground from which it sprung was abandoned concrete; cold dark alleys, with shadows and crannies that play host to folks who have been banned from the majestic, modern cathedrals that host many believers on Sunday. But much like the persistent shrubs that push through cracks in the sidewalks, a slow careful movement of the Spirit brought together a hotchpotch collection of outcasts.

In the early years, Metro gatherings consisted of a few 'recovering Pharisees', convicted by the cries contained within a desperate email, determined to explore a richer ecclesial practice, and a larger group of the street-connected community: folks struggling with addiction and mental health issues, girls working the street, the homeless, all in desperate need of a gospel that worked. We borrowed space from the local homeless shelter, using their hall for gatherings and fellowship, hosting dinners, and musical café-style events. Many among us who had no home would use this time to sleep, sometimes as a side-effect of narcotics or prescription medications.

As we explored our sense of vocation, we soon discovered that God in his mercy loved to humble the proud, by powerfully, repeatedly and profoundly speaking through the least likely among us. This realization began a process of formulating the beginnings of a rule of life; disciplines, rhythms, distinctively "local" theology and values that persist to this day, subject to the Spirit's voice, but held with tremendous reverence.

At an early stage in the formation of our community, a young man approached me. He was difficult to engage as he struggled with a lack of social skills and desperately craved attention. My impatience and selfish nature led me to avoid him, hardly the heart of a shepherd! On this occasion I could find no escape, and listened as he shared with me his observations of our Metro Community. Dan had some form of learning disorder, and frequently repeated himself. He had been observing the growth of the community and he felt that it was all about four things: "seeking God, pursuing truth, in an atmosphere of love, where judgment was left at the door." Dan offered us our mission statement. To this day, these remain the foundations of Metro. Dan helped me realize that God loves to reveal his character and Kingdom through those on the edges – the outsiders.

"The Church is only the church, when it exists for others." – Dietrich Bonheoffer

Discovering Brokenness

The hall at the local shelter was now full, and we were in need of a larger venue. The nightclub across the street seemed like a reasonable "third space" and in need of redemptive activity. Our community was slightly enamored by the opportunity because most nights the bouncers barred our folks from entering, deeming them unworthy of participating -- but also because they could rarely afford the cover charge.

It also seemed somewhat logical, as Sunday mornings were hardly busy times for the owner. And on Easter Sunday in 2006 we launched a gathering with a breakfast for the entire street community. These meals became a feature and value for us: hospitality is our practice. But the biggest surprise that day began as numerous middle-class people streamed in the door. Protective of our merry, eclectic band, I feared that this might be the ruin of all that God was doing, but it became clear that poverty and brokenness of spirit is no respecter of wallet or social status, and that God had plans of his own: perhaps I had not being paying attention.

Some came, seeking to be among those "more screwed-up" than they were (or so they perceived). Others came to be invisible. Still others came to "help the poor." buoyed by a romanticized sense of being among those forced to live in the margins. Our community has learned to deal with all these heart attitudes with patience and grace. The most astonishing revelation is that the ministers of grace are often those whom we deem in need of saving. Living and serving the outsiders of society is not easy; a consequence of the conditions of our hearts, rather than the people themselves.

Brennan Manning in his book, *The Ragamuffin Gospel,* says, "The deeper we grow in the spirit of Jesus Christ, the poorer we become – the more we rejoice that everything in life is a gift … Awareness of our poverty and ineptitude causes us to rejoice in the gift of being called out of darkness into wondrous light and translated into the Kingdom of God's beloved Son."[3]

True community, in the image of a God who is community, cannot and must not be a place where people are allowed to be invisible. The powerful notion of belonging is by very definition a recognition of value and worth. All in our community have experienced this. Those with a street-connected background know what it means to be relegated to shadows and alleys while the rest of the world passes them by. I have stood with my friends on the street watching people cross to the other side to avoid contact with us. The poverty of relationship is akin to being invisible.

Yet being invisible is not the preserve of the poor. Many cloistered behind their suburban fences and sitting week after week in the same pew in the yawning sanctuary have encountered a poverty of relationship, loneliness, and a sense of isolation that rivals that of the outcast. Henri Nouwen writes,

> When we are not afraid to confess our own poverty, we will be able to be with other people in theirs. The Christ who lives in our own poverty recognizes the Christ who lives in other peoples. Just as we are inclined to ignore our own poverty, we are inclined to ignore others'. We prefer not to see people who are destitute, we do not like to look at people who are deformed or disabled, we avoid talking about people's pains and sorrows, we stay away from brokenness, helplessness, and neediness.

> By this avoidance we might lose touch with the people through whom God is manifested to us. But when we have discovered God

in our own poverty, we will lose our fear of the poor and go to them to meet God.[4]

Imago Dei

It's in this notion of belonging that we discover that we are all equal. The journey of discovery towards living out the truth that we are made in God's image and therefore all worthy of love, dignity and relationship, is a rocky one, because we are sinful, selfish creatures. Shame is a cancer on the streets of our city, and allowed to run rampant in the shadows of our buildings and the lives of our community. The enemy has been tremendously effective in convincing people from all walks of life that they are not worthy of God's love.

However broken a person is through life's trauma, God's image in them remains. We therefore need to treat all people with dignity. In this effort the Church has done a terrible disservice among the poor in Canada. As people join the Metro Community, they are typically cynical and negative in their experience of the rules, rituals and routines of organized religion. This isn't reserved to the experience of First Nations people in relation to residential schools, but is common to the poor at the hands of Evangelicalism. The pervasive view of the Church from the fringes is her concern with a "soul-winning" dualism that ignores the call to shalom: to justice and wholeness and reconciliation: her call to be among "the least of these." Without a willingness to place action alongside words[5] that speak to body and spirit we fail to recognize the personhood of the One we wish to serve, and so are fail to reflect God's nature. Our mandate in loving God's world (John 3:16-17) is a mandate to reflect God.

"For several centuries," Manning writes, "the Celtic church of Ireland was spared the Greek dualism of matter and spirit. They regarded the world with the clear vision of faith. When a young Celtic monk saw his cat catch a salmon swimming in shallow water, he cried, 'The power of the Lord is in the paw of the cat!'"[6]

Metro Central

Our community center at Metro is the hub for many social agencies in our city to connect with those struggling with poverty, mental illness and addiction. Wednesday evenings have become significant moments to build community, to connect with those on the edges of society and to invite them in.

On one such Wednesday evening I was walking through the downtown with a member of our community who had a long history with heroin. I had come to enjoy his company, not least because he had an uncanny knack for sniffing out trouble, but because he had discernment: he could tell a lie from truth immediately. Steve had been an enforcer for the Hell's Angels; all 310 pounds of his frame had been dedicated to inflicting pain on unfortunate souls who got in his way.

This night we bumped into two young men in their early twenties, clearly nervous being in the downtown after dark. They had been wandering through the streets, randomly asking those who seemed homeless, if they wished to "be saved." Many had in earnest answered yes, for whom they had then prayed, informed them that the Holy Spirit had indeed saved them – from addiction, poverty, and their sin. Then they would simply move on. We had encountered a few of their "victims" already that evening, and so somewhat hot under the collar, I began to ask them what they were doing? They said, "We have been sent by our church to save the souls of these people."

I asked them, "So, how do my friends know then that God loves them? What happens next?"

"Well, that's not really our responsibility," they replied. "We were told to free them in prayer. The rest is God's job."

It is interesting that in Scripture we see that Jesus spends as much time helping the physically sick as dealing with spiritual sickness. In Colossians 3:9-10 we are told that reconnecting with God means that we can all be renewed in his likeness. Paul goes on in this passage to talk about how people, in spite of their differences, have become a new community. God loves diversity! And imperfection is not a hindrance. The weaker member is more needful (1 Corinthians 12). The church is characterized by people who remain imperfect, yet by the Spirit create a fellowship that is attractive and welcoming to all: where the stranger is the treasured guest.

One of the values we hold at Metro is a commitment to understanding poverty in all its forms. There is no question that there is an economic dimension to poverty, but for many the pain of circumstance and situation runs deeper than a lack of resources and possessions. Poverty has to do with status, choice, opportunity, dignity, justice, relationship, community, and hope.

"The central thrust of biblical teaching on economic activity is that everyone should enjoy the benefits that accrue from it. In this sphere Old Testament law, prophetic announcements and the teaching of Jesus and his disciples are very much biased towards the poor."[7]

In real and practical terms, we seek to live out God's principles of "tenancy and stewardship." God explains to us that our approach and posture must be that of tenants. We do not own God's creation: we are merely stewards of it. This radically shifts our sharing of resources and how we invite others into that tenancy.

At Metro the notion of redemption, rescue, and restoration are values that carry immediate power for those who have lost hope. God's principles of the Year of Jubilee are amazing in their practicality. The reality is that people will become poor, but this is not a judgment upon them. We have begun to ask questions of what a church community might look like where poverty does not become a trap from which people cannot escape. We need special grace for those who have become poor, to guard and ensure their dignity.

The welfare system in Canada is lauded as a matter of pride, but the reality is that it often serves as a trap. The cycle of dependency allows people to merely survive, rather than thrive. The voices of the most vulnerable have served as the mouthpiece for justice in this regard, causing us to venture into the risky realm of social enterprise. Over the last three years, Metro has launched a coffee shop, moving company, commercial laundry business, and a financial literacy foundation, all of which employ members of our community, restoring dignity and providing meaningful work. These enterprises have helped to break the chains of unworthiness, a first step in restoration and deep healing.

Justice for the poor is the responsibility of the entire community. Moreover, our understanding of poverty cannot be limited to simple materialism. Much like the first century, our community experiences poverty financially, but also socially, spiritually, physically and politically – and all these are interrelated (as seen in Luke 4). Bryant Myers describes poverty as "a result of relationships that do not work, that are not just, that are not for life, that are not harmonious or enjoyable. Poverty is the absence of shalom in all its meanings."[8]

Community – "Being home," not just "having a home"

"Probably no word better summarizes the suffering of our times than the word 'homeless.' It reveals one of our deepest and most painful conditions, the conditions of not having a place where we can feel safe, cared for, protected and loved."[9]

As I write, snow falls on the streets of our city as temperatures fall below freezing. As Tom, one of the hope-givers and pastoral leaders at Metro opened the doors this morning, some forty-five people poured through the doors. We began our day in prayer: a rhythm that has taken root amongst us, a deep necessity.

Hundreds of pairs of feet wander through the door each day. Many come early for the anchoring rhythm of prayer and a brief connection. Some stay, using the art studio, laundry, computers, music studio, clothing room. Some simply hang out in the coffee shop, and slump into the couches of one of the few 'living rooms' that make up our home. By noon, the aroma of home cooking makes its way from the community kitchen where Brian, a dear white-haired, grandfatherly soul affectionately known as "Pops," heads the operation to feed the ones who will sit down for fellowship at lunch.

Pops was a drug addict for most of his adult life. Brian defies the odds for survival. With the academic abilities of a third-grader, he never read a word of the Bible. Embarrassed by his inability to read, he learnt ways of covering up his shame. In his frustration and anger, he was quick to fight, and had served a number of stints behind bars. A radical encounter with Christ and the enduring love and constant care of a number of souls in our community have seen a new man emerge.

In the early days of Metro, I would find an inebriated Brian, mumbling and stammering so badly on a street corner that he was virtually unintelligible. Years on, my heart soars as he shares at our Sunday "open mic," speaking clearly and boldly of his love for Jesus. He has learned to read God's Word, and his newfound dignity and peace shines in his life. I watch as he gazes thoughtfully at the people he lovingly considers his children.

"The opposite of poverty is not wealth. The opposite of both poverty and wealth is community."[10]

Absence of community is the most crippling aspect of poverty, but it's invisible. Poverty of relationship is poverty of the soul. When you take away relationship, you take away the essence of being human, our very connection with the triune God, the One who is community.

There is much to be said of the values, rhythms, and journey of an urban church plant, particularly an unusual one such as ours. We share stories of striving for wholeness, stories of change and empowerment, stories of loss and unspeakable grief and unbelievable joy – in equal measure. These require a journey into mystery and tension, living in that tension and living with others in the mess and chaos of their lives, constantly dying to oneself, and pointing to Jesus.

"Clutter and mess show us that life is being lived ... Tidiness makes me think of held breath, of suspended animation ... Perfectionism is a mean, frozen form of idealism, while messes are the artist's true friend. What people somehow forgot to mention when we were children was that we need to make messes in order to find out who we are and why we are here."[11]

Being Present

Born in the 60s as a flower child shaped the way Kathryn has lived much of her life. A bohemian spirit, in the guise of a small delicate pixie-like frame, it's easy to misjudge or dismiss her, as she collects cans and sings to herself in a gravelly voice. A few years ago I began to get to know her in a way that has genuinely changed my life and my heart. I often imagine what she might have been like in the hazy summers of San Francisco. Her love of all things floral, and her passion for having the last word, conjure up images of a headstrong young woman in a time of shifting cultural realities.

Some fifty years on, the survivor of a vibrant but destructive lifestyle, chasing bands like The Doors, Jimi Hendrix and The Eagles (she has pictures to prove it) Kathryn found her way to Canada, became a Nurse/Care Aide, eventually married, and settled down. Social alcoholism blew up into full-blown addiction when marital problems emerged, and excruciating back pain from an accident, as well as two life-threatening bouts of cancer, led to an all-encompassing addiction to pain-killers. For a number of years she has rotated on and off the street.

One warm summer afternoon, as we stood in the art studio at Metro Central, Kathryn told me her story. And as she did so, I was powerfully aware that I was no longer meeting with just her, but there was a tangible sense that Jesus was present as well. As she tearfully told me her life story, I began to realize the strength and depth of this incredible woman. To my horror, as she described the pain she had endured, she lifted her shirt to reveal two jagged ugly scars where her breasts once had been. Her emaciated chest was boyish and her wrinkled skin stretched taut over protruding ribs and diminutive frame.

In one quick instant, I felt both guilt for fearing the reaction of anyone who might stumble in, and wonder at the awkward gift of a moment like this. I felt deeply honored for her vulnerable trust.

The gift of time, "being present" with people, is a two-way gift. That day, Kathryn welcomed me into a trusted place of friendship, but in her and through her I also encountered Jesus. That moment began an enduring and meaningful friendship. As the church of Jesus, and as individuals, we are each faced with two profound truths. Firstly, that God sent his Son to be among us. And secondly, my capacity to be the presence of Jesus will require that I too be sent, sent to live among the people of my community.

Being present is a discipline we seek to practice at Metro. It's a countercultural position and a counter-personal posture. My will seeks to dominate: the Spirit emancipates. My will tends to destroy and consume: the Spirit continually creates. My will defends: the Spirit calls me to vulnerability.

As a community we are discovering the beauty of encountering Jesus in the most unexpected places. This discovery is always a battle. In a culture like ours, there is constant chaos on the streets and in the lives of the ones we call family, the ones we love. We must guard against the misdirection of the enemy. Satan has us looking to our right, when

Jesus appears to our left. Busy trying to be Jesus to others, we miss him for a number of reasons:

- His transcendence. We're looking down, caught up in the "tyranny of the urgent."
- His humanity. We find ourselves asking, "How could he be so ordinary?"
- His brokenness, in which he is present, tempts us to draw away.

Powerlessness and humility in the spiritual life do not refer to people who have no spine and who let everyone else make decisions for them. They refer to people who are so deeply in love with Jesus that they are ready to follow him wherever he guides them, always trusting that with him, they will find life and find it abundantly.[12]

A theology that is "Distinctly Local"

Eugene Peterson speaks of "all discipleship being local,"[13] that it is worked out in particular places, whether rural, suburban or urban, along roads and streets and avenues and beside real flesh-and-blood neighbours. In other words, we simply cannot work out our faith dislocated from the world around us. Place and context matter. A unique part of the Metro journey is the realization that God in his mercy has allowed us to develop a theology that is distinctly local. We are deeply aware of our geography, the urban-ness and "now-ness" of the culture of our fellow brothers and sisters. This is evidenced by the emerging movement of the middle-class members of our community from the suburbs to the downtown core.

Agricultural metaphors are ones that resonate with us. In much the same way that Wendell Berry or Eugene Peterson would speak of the need to "understand the soil," we find ourselves up to our necks in the virtually untilled soil of an urban landscape. And yet God is on the move. A long winter is giving way to spring, and young shoots are springing up. Renewal, restoration and redemption are enriching the soil, and new life is emerging in fields where once all hope was lost. God is answering our prayer: "Your kingdom come, on earth as it is in heaven."

About Laurence East

Laurence East grew up in a village in India and moved to Cyprus and Europe as a teenager. A product of boarding school and with an insatiable appetite for travel, Laurence found adventure in China, Tibet, India and all over South America, but managed to pick up an MA in Political Science from the University of London (SOAS) along the way. Laurence, his wife Sarah and their three multi-culturally confused kids have been a part of the Metro Community in downtown Kelowna from its inception.

Bibliography

Hughes, Dewi. *God of the Poor: A Biblical Vision of God's Present Rule.* Carlisle: OM, 1998.

Lamott, Anne. *Bird by Bird: Some Instructions on Writing and Life.* New York: Anchor, 1995.

Manning, Brennan. *The Ragamuffin Gospel: Good News for the Bedraggled, Beat-Up, and Burnt Out.* Colorado Springs: Multnomah, 2005.

Nouwen, Henri. *Reaching Out: The Three Movements of the Spiritual Life.* New York: Doubleday, 1986.

_____. *In the Name of Jesus: Reflections on Christian Leadership.* New York: The Crossroad Publishing Company, 1992.

Peterson, Eugene. *Christ Plays in Ten Thousand Places: A Conversation in Spiritual Theology.* Grand Rapids: William B. Eerdmans, 2005.

Stott, John R.W. *Issues Facing Christians.* Grand Rapids: Zondervan, 2006.

1 Not their real names.

2 Stott, *Issues Facing Christians.*

3 Manning, *The Ragamuffin Gospel.*

4 Nouwen, "Meditations."

5 James 2:14-17

6 *The Ragamuffin Gospel.*

7 Hughes, *God of the Poor*, 157.

8 Myers, *Walking with the Poor*, 86

9 Nouwen, *Reaching Out*.

10 Ibid.

11 Lamott, *Bird by Bird*.

12 Nouwen, *In the Name of Jesus*, 84.

13 Peterson, *Christ Plays in Ten Thousand Places*, 72.

Chapter 10

God is the Interesting Thing: Saint Benedict's Table, Winnipeg

Jamie Howison

The invitation to do some focused writing around the shape and nature of our church community is a welcome one, in that it is always a useful and healthy thing for a pastoral leader to take a few steps back from day-to-day ministry in order to offer some reflection around what it is that we think we are doing. At the same time, I find it a fairly daunting prospect to attempt to convey, from what amounts to a standing start, what it is that we've been about these past five years.

I'm almost inclined to say that if you really want to get a feel for what we're about, what you'll really need to do is to come and join us for a Sunday liturgy, one of our monthly Saturday evening contemplative services, maybe a session in our ideaExchange series that we hold in this great little used book store, and then arrange to go for coffee so that I can fill in the blanks, offer you some ideas for reading, and pass along a copy of our CD of the original music that has been written from within the context of the community. Maybe after doing all of those things, what I have written here will actually come close to successfully describing life at Saint Benedict's Table. Wishful thinking,

I know, but it does speak to just how hard it is to convey much of a church community's life with just words on paper.

The other challenge, though, has to do with whether I'm writing this as a "church planter" or as a pastoral leader of a community that is making the move from "traditional to emergent; attractional to missional." Those are the broad categories which Len suggested in the invitation to contribute to this book, and while I suspect many of the other contributors will find it relatively clear which of the two best describes their situation, in the case of our community that fit is less clear.[1]

Yes, we are a new church plant – which brings a kind of freedom but also a whole series of challenges, the least of which was not financial in our earliest days – but we are also a "mission" of the Anglican Diocese of Rupert's Land, and so live within a very specific ecclesial and liturgical context. This too comes with its particular challenges, but it too brings what must also be described as a freedom; freedom from having to steadily re-invent the proverbial wheel, but also freedom from the kind of anomie or normlessness that can sometimes hamstring a new or renewing community as it seeks to find its identity.

We stand, for instance, within the 450-year liturgical heritage of the Anglican tradition, which means much more than just a towering stack of dusty prayer books and hymnals. There is a continuous line which connects what we do in our Eucharistic worship with what our forebears have been doing for centuries, a line which takes us right back to the visionary reforming work of Thomas Cranmer, the chief architect of the English Book of Common Prayer. This tradition is much, much more than just a set of liturgical texts which can be implemented (or not) by the local church. It is a heritage which is at once liturgical, spiritual and theological, providing a context within which both the corporate body and the individual believer live out the faith. Now to be sure, our community's liturgical texts and habits are quite different from what Archbishop Cranmer envisioned in the first prayer book of 1549, but there is a continuity which grounds and anchors us, a continuity which stretches back to and includes the great tradition of the early Church fathers on which the prayer book is itself grounded.

From time to time, someone will ask why it is that we have "placed ourselves within the Anglican structure," almost as if we went shopping for a denomination and decided to pick this one as our home location;

the implication, of course, is that if need or circumstance made it prudent we could do a denominational switch. Our reality is actually quite different from this, in that Saint Benedict's Table is a local manifestation of the Body of Christ as that is construed and lived out within an Anglican context. We are, in short, Anglican.

On a practical level, this means that we live our ministry and life within a tradition with certain marks, with a particular identity. When in the late 1800's it had become abundantly clear that the Anglican tradition had expanded far beyond its earlier identity as the Church of England, the 1888 Lambeth Conference of bishops from around the Communion approved four points by which it marked itself as a Communion:

- The Holy Scriptures of the Old and New Testaments, as "containing all things necessary for salvation", and as being the rule and ultimate standard of faith.
- The Apostles' Creed, as the Baptismal Symbol; and the Nicene Creed, as the sufficient statements of the Christian Faith.
- The two Sacraments ordained by Christ Himself – Baptism and the Supper of the Lord – ministered with unfailing use of Christ's Words of Institution, and of the elements ordained by Him.
- The Historic Episcopate, locally adapted in the methods of its administration to the varying needs of the nations and peoples called of God into the Unity of His Church.[2]

This, then, is our context. Whatever we might do anew – in whatever ways we might seek to recapitulate the tradition – is always grounded in this foundation.

As I mentioned above, Saint Benedict's Table is designated as a mission of the Diocese of Rupert's Land in the Anglican Church of Canada. While we have had this official canonical status since October 2004, the community began to be birthed in the spring of 2003, when a small group of a dozen or so people began to meet bi-weekly for Sunday evening worship. In part inspired by the so-called "emergent church" movement, this group was gathered around a desire to explore the possibility of forming a worshipping community both rooted in the liturgical and theological resources of Anglicanism and open to new expressions which might flow from that tradition. Borrowing a phrase from Robert Webber, we began to describe ourselves as being "rooted in an ancient-future."[3]

It is notable that right from the start our worship, which uses a simple liturgy adapted from the Canadian Book of Alternative Services, was centred around the table. So much so, in fact, that when in August 2003 we made the decision to move to weekly gatherings on an ongoing basis, the choice of the word "table" in our name was both spontaneous and unanimous. Further, that St Benedict was chosen as the patron was in part due to the Benedictine emphasis on hospitality, on welcoming each guest as Christ.

For the first 10 months or so of weekly gatherings, we met on Sunday evenings at St Alban's Church, a small and attractive parish building in an urban residential neighbourhood in Winnipeg. Because at the time I was still serving as the pastor of a combined Anglican and Lutheran church community in a Winnipeg suburb, there was a real sense that our gatherings were really just explorations of a possible future together, rather than a fully realized church plant. In fact, because I was more or less "moonlighting" with Saint Benedict's Table, we didn't advertise ourselves widely or really do much together beyond our Sunday evening liturgies.

Still, by the end of that 10-month period we had a steady congregation of some 45 people on most Sunday evenings, and a respectable projected offering income of some $45,000 for the coming year. This put us in a position of being able to seriously contemplate seeking some seed money from the diocese, in order that we might formalize our status as a new mission, thus allowing me to move into full-time stipendiary ministry. While the diocese did not see itself able to provide such funding, All Saints' Church in downtown Winnipeg stepped in to offer a grant of $20,000 a year for two years, and invited us in to their building rent-free. The understanding was that we would stay on at All Saints for a third year, and that if possible we would at that point begin to share some of the costs of ministry in that space. The move to All Saints was made in June 2004, with the grant funding beginning in January 2005. I moved into full-time ministry on the first Sunday of Advent 2004, just over a month after we received official status as a mission of the diocese.

We have now finished our first three years at All Saints – actually, three and a half if you include the six months we were there prior to the beginning of our grant period – and as we had hoped we were able to pay a monthly rental/shared ministry fee of $1000 during the third year. We have extended our sharing agreement by an additional three years, and are currently exploring how we might increase our "ownership" in the parish building. To this end, we have been given a good-sized meeting and program room for our own use, and have begun to explore ways in which we might profitably share some aspects of ministry with the All Saints congregation. The intention here is not to meld the two communities, as they are quite distinct in terms of congregational culture and general ethos, but rather to find ways in which the two communities might support and uphold each other as we share some of our life together.

Aside from worship, virtually everything else we do is carried on outside of the walls of the church, and we believe that is as it should be. There are two book groups that meet over breakfast in local restaurants, a weekly home-based Bible study, a monthly educational event held in a used book store, occasional pub evenings ("Theology by the Glass"), and various other points of connection for the community, yet worship is utterly central to all that we are and all that we do. We have continued our pattern of gathering in the evening on Sundays for Eucharistic worship, and have also added a monthly Saturday evening contemplative liturgy of the word called "Hear the Silence."

All Saints' Church is of neo-Gothic design, configured with a high altar, chancel and rood-screen, with fixed pews seating 450. Pews have been removed from the front, making possible the use of a nave altar. We use a small carved oak table, placed in front of the chancel stairs, as our altar. The presider sits in the front pew, oriented to the table along with the community. The lessons are read from a lectern placed midway down the aisle, and the sermon is usually preached from the middle of the aisle at the front.

The liturgy follows a fairly conventional flow: 1) the community is gathered; 2) the Word is proclaimed and prayer is offered; 3) communion is shared; and, 4) the community is sent out into the world, rejoicing in the power of the Holy Spirit. We continue to use a somewhat simplified version of the communion rite from the Book of Alternative Services, and our basic liturgical text is reproduced in colour from hand-drawn illuminated originals, which are placed in restaurant menu covers and accompanied by a sheet with the music and variable prayers for the week. These coloured "liturgy cards," which have been drawn for us by a gifted member of the community, vary seasonally.

There is nothing particularly startling about the shape of that worship, yet within the basic structure we seek less conventional ways in which to draw the community into a place of openness to the presence of God. The musicians, for instance, remain seated and off to the side. They do not face the congregation, but rather with the congregation are oriented toward the communion table. Though there are different ensembles of players, there is generally a guitar or two, a bass, sometimes a percussionist and often a pianist. The music tends to be meditative, much in the vein of France's monastic Taize community, though written and played with a little more grit and feel; many of our musicians have roots music backgrounds, and it shows.

On Sundays at 7:00pm, the main church bell is sounded and the music just begins. People put down the coffee they had picked up at the back of the church, and make their way quietly to their places to join in the singing. As the music resolves, a sounding bowl is rung and incense is lit as a sign of our ascending prayer. We've learned to let the stillness linger for as long as the bowl resounds; to not rush, as if the quiet is somehow offensive. This is followed by the formal liturgical greeting, which varies seasonally and which bridges us into another piece of music. Depending on the season, this might be in the vein of the traditional *Gloria*; celebratory and marked by a powerful sense of alleluia.

It might be something like a Wesley hymn, recreated by our musicians to feel more earthy and perhaps more evocative, or an original piece by one of our songwriters. Regardless, the focus is on the gathering of this community, to begin to make us ready to hear the Word and share the cup.

Prayer is offered, using the collect prayer appointed for that particular day, and then readings from scripture are shared. We do follow the Revised Common Lectionary, but tend to use just the appointed Gospel lesson and one of the other two readings. The reading is unrushed, surrounded by silence, and done from a lectern placed in the middle of the congregation. A sermon of no longer than 10 or 12

an unlikely icon for the triune nature of the One; we have always shared sherry and shortbread off the communion table at the very end of the Christmas Eve liturgy as a very visceral reminder that such Holy Days are in fact feast days. Last year we added "mimosas" (sparkling wine and orange juice) to our Easter Day celebrations, and to the delight of the children I fired the cork from the first bottle right to the back of the church, accompanied by a hearty "Alleluia! Christ is Risen!" But those are the festal exceptions to the rule; usually we let the music and stillness, the icons and incense, the bread and wine, the words and prayers, do their work.

In the space at the back of the church is another table which also shapes who and what we are: the table of refreshment. Each week as worship closes, we invite people to gather at that table of hospitality and to share a bit of life over coffee and food. That the church is anchored by twin tables is not accidental, for what the community does at one must be mirrored in the other.[5] Close to that hospitality table are the large baskets for the fruit and vegetables which have been brought as donations to the soup kitchen. These four baskets, which are filled to overflowing each week, when brought forward with the bread and wine are placed at the base of the communion table.

Again, this is not an accidental thing, that when the community comes forward to feast at the table we see our symbolic offering in the name of the One who called the poor and the hungry blessed. The community is regularly reminded that we should not imagine that a few baskets of fruit will solve the world's hunger and absolve us from responsibility. The baskets are a sacramental thing – a prophetic act directed at ourselves – which keep reminding us that to dare to feast at this table is to be made deeply, even uncomfortably aware of the abiding hunger of the world.

The cumulative effect of this way of celebrating communion is to emphasize our common life together before God. Though certain people are entrusted with roles of leadership – lectors, intercessors, musicians, communion administrants, and not least of all the presider, who is the sole person vested in worship – all are united in our orientation as a people together before God. The open invitation to share in the bread and wine, quite literally around the table in community, is for many a point of entry – or re-entry for those who may have found themselves distanced or alienated from the church of their upbringing - into this local manifestation of the Body of Christ. As the following attestations from members of our community will suggest, there is certainly a personal dimension to this participation, but it is one set very much in a corporate context:

> Gathering the community around the table reminds me that I am not alone and that it truly is God who has invited us to the table of our Lord. Receiving these gifts from members of the community reminds me that we are all called to be servants of God. – T.B.

> The offering of bread and wine one-to-one personalizes the experience, the common cup reinforces the communal aspect, and the offering of the elements by people other than a pastor/elder/deacon reminds of the equality of all in Christ. – A.B.

> The free, open coming together at the communion table in front of the church to celebrate the death, resurrection and presence of Christ in the midst of us at that moment filled me with a deep sense of wonder, peace, joy and oneness with all people. There was no exclusion; neither was there any judgment; no prying into myself by other more mature Christians; no shame felt during confession, no sense of 'you don't belong because you are not the same as, or as good as, or as right as. One requirement only – hunger. – M.D.

> Pass the cup around
> I can hardly speak a word,
> And I am lost;
> Pass the bread around
> I cannot sustain my self,
> The day is growing longer;
> Every time I come back to this table
> I think ... I might believe ...
> We might believe
> We long to feast
> We might believe ...
> "Pass the Cup Around" ©Jenny Moore, 2005

It should be noted that our practice is one of what is called "open table," in which the invitation to communion is extended to all who would feel called. There is no requirement that participants be regular attenders at our gatherings or even that they be baptized; rather the single requirement is that a person feel open to, and hungry for, this way of encountering the living Christ in the midst of his Body, the church. Our invitation to communion, adapted from one used in the Iona Community of Scotland, states our theology clearly:

> This is the table, not merely of the church, but of Christ
> It is made ready for those who love him
> and for those who want to love him more.
> So come, whether you have much faith or little;
> whether you have tried to follow,
> or are afraid you have failed.
> Come, because it is Christ who invites you.
> It is his will that those who want to meet him might meet him here.

Further, we are quite clear that the hospitable opening of the communion table is not merely a pastoral default setting, but rather a theologically informed choice. Though there is not the space here to lay out this position in detail, we understand our practice of open table to be embedded in the very ethos of our church community, central to our identity as a local manifestation of the Body of Christ.[6]

Sometime in the late 1930s, Evelyn Underhill – a highly respected scholar working in the area of Christian spirituality and mysticism – wrote a letter to the Archbishop of Canterbury of her day, outlining what she saw as being crucial for the regeneration of the spiritual life and integrity of the Church of England. "God is the interesting thing," she wrote, and went on to call for the Church to withdraw from any activity in which God had somehow been pushed to the margins. Her message was for the clergy to get out of the helping profession – to stop trying to justify their existence as some sort of sanctified social workers – and for the church to drop any pretense of being a club or some generally helpful community agency. If "God is the interesting thing," then the church is first and foremost to be about the worship of God and the cultivation of a people who desire to be steeped in prayer, meditation and study.

The Archbishop's response goes unrecorded. In fact, there is no way to be sure that the letter was actually ever sent. In our church community, however, we have taken Underhill's challenge very seriously. We've been at this coming on five years now, and we're just beginning to discover just how deep those basic building blocks can take us; deep into the mystery of God.

And God is the interesting thing.

Portions of this chapter appeared in different forms in "Come to the Table," published by Saint Benedict's Table, and in vol. 4, num. 19 of the online magazine *Catapult*.

About Jamie Howison

Jamie Howison is a priest in the Anglican Church of Canada, and the founding pastor of Saint Benedict's Table in Winnipeg. He has worked in full-time ministry in a variety of contexts for over 20 years, but is just now beginning to realize that his knees are too old to play soccer and his taste in music has made a definitive shift, as is evidenced in his move from a subscription to Rolling Stone to now reading Downbeat. The original vision for saint benedict's table was dreamed up in a conversation with his wife, Catherine Pate, while riding the Long Island Railway on the way back from spending two days studying theology with Robert Farrar Capon.

Bibliography

Cross, F.L., and E.A. Livingstone. *The Oxford Dictionary of the Christian Church.* New York: Oxford University Press, 1983.

Fitch, David E., and Geoff Holsclaw. *Prodigal Christianity: 10 Signposts into the Missional Frontier.* San Francisco: Jossey-Bass, 2013.

Webber, Robert. *Ancient-Future Faith: Rethinking Evangelicalism for a Postmodern World.* Grand Rapids: Baker, 1999.

1 See also David Fitch's new book with Geoff Holsclaw, *Prodigal Christianity*, where they suggest that the primary features of post-Christendom with which new initiatives must content are defined by post-attractional, post-positional (authority) and post-universal.

2 Cross, *The Oxford Dictionary of the Christian Church.*

3 Webber, *Ancient-Future Faith.*

4 To pass a plate is to look to guests and visitors to bolster the community's budget, which is deeply problematic. Instead, we have a basket for offerings on the table at the back of the church, and our assumption is that those who wish to make a donation will do so.

5 I am aware that at innovative Church of St Gregory of Nyssa in San Francisco the refreshments are served from the communion table, which is an even more blatant way of connecting the table of communion to the other tables in our lives. Aside from Christmas Eve, when sherry and shortbread are served from our communion table at the end of the liturgy, we have found it more helpful to think in terms of the ways in which all of the tables at which we gather – including the table at the back of the nave, but also those in the coffee shops, in our homes, and at the local pub – mirror and echo the communion table.

6 For a detailed outline of this position, see *Come to the Table*, a small book published by our community and available through our website: www.stbenedictstable.ca

Chapter 11

The Open Door, Montreal
Kim Reid

My name is Kim Reid, I was born in Kingston, Ontario, but have spent most of my life in the Montreal area. I was born into a family that did not place any importance on following Jesus, so I was introduced to Jesus through foster parents. My only experience with church before this was occasionally attending an Anglican church, whose minister had an affection for alcohol and picked his sermons out of a file right before the morning service. Kids ate toast and peanut butter in the front rows, men read the paper in the back. It was a vibrant little church. We used to steal snow shovels and store them in the church boiler room. The janitor could never figure out why he had 15 shovels.

My last experience in a foster home was with Christian (Pentecostal) foster parents. I was 12, and not very interested in church. They did not force me and my brother to go to church, and somewhere along the line this made me curious. When I began going, I was pretty freaked out by the expressiveness of the people. There was a lot of cultural real estate between my little Anglican church and this massive Pentecostal church.

I have never fit in to the church culture. Even when I was in my early teens, I always felt a little outside. When I was young, I thought this was a bad thing. I tried to fit in, but I am not very good at faking it. I never quite understood the fortress mentality of many evangelical churches. They seem to be protecting themselves from my friends and family, who weren't that dangerous.

I skipped around denominations a lot in my late teens and developed what I called back then a denominational tolerance and appreciation. I would say that if we could take the good from most denoms and put them together we might have a pretty amazing church.

After high school, I began working with marginalized people; first, with the intellectually handicapped and later on with juvenile delinquents. I had always sensed that I would be in full-time ministry, but I didn't know what that would look like because I did NOT want to be a pastor. Back in the early 70's, if you were in ministry, you were a pastor.

In my experience working with delinquents, I started to envision being an influence in kids' lives before they were "in the system." I started dreaming about this drop-in center idea.

In 1986, I married Sylvia. In 1991, God made it clear to us that it was time to move into the next chapter of our lives. I made it clear to Him that He needed to tell Syl this as well. Turned out He was already doing it. I approached Youth For Christ with this drop-in center idea, only to find out that they operated a few such centers across Canada. Why reinvent the wheel? The process of joining YFC began.

In 1992, The Vault opened. I was in ministry heaven. Little did I know that God was having fun. Through the Vault, we have seen many lives change, most for the better. We have watched "kids" grow in faith and become true Jesus followers. Some have gone into full-time ministry.

I realized from the beginning that the key to reaching people and changing lives was long-term involvement. That meant we needed staff that would stick around. The average drop-in staff stay at the time was about six months. We decided that our staff would need to be a cohesive group of people with a single-minded purpose, and a sense that they were in this together. So,we became a family. We poured our lives into each other. We played, prayed, laughed and cried together. We loved each other and our kids, and the kids knew it. We began referring to ourselves as "the community."

We would work the drop-in on Friday and Saturday nights, and hang out at my house on Sunday nights. We would watch movies, eat, play games and just have fun. This became known as the open house at Kim & Syl's. After a while other people started showing up. "I heard there was an open house here tonight: is anybody welcome?" Sometimes we didn't even know the people. We had to change the format because we couldn't afford to feed thirty people every week. So, we would get people to bring ingredients for the "meal." Syl would decide what we were going to eat. People would phone in and she would tell them what component to bring and the meal would come together.

Somewhere along the way, people started feeling the need for more than just movies and games. People started talking about worshipping on Sunday nights before food and movies. So,we pulled out a few guitars and worshipped. A few months down the road and people started expressing the need for sharing Scripture and learning. So we pulled out some Bibles and started sharing Scripture together.

I have always been frustrated with the chasm that exists between the reality of my world and the people I hang with, and the subculture of the Church. As I spent more and more time with unchurched people, I realized that our little world made no sense outside of the church walls. This is why people don't want to be a part of our little game; it makes no sense in the real world. As our ministry grew it made less sense to me as well.

At this point I was an elder in a church with Brethren roots. The church was quite progressive for an evangelical church, but still did not connect with the people we were meeting.

In 2002, a little before Christmas, I asked our Sunday night group what they got out of church. All 30 of us had the same answer: nothing. Sunday church was where we meet each other, and begin our day together. People weren't connecting with the music or the message being communicated in the more formal setting. So why get up at 9 a.m. to be at church for 11 a.m., when you only went to bed at 3 a.m.?

While this was going on, I was getting the sinking feeling that we were a church already. That God had played a sick joke on me, and had created a church while I wasn't paying attention.

Early in 2003, we received an invitation to a church planting congress in Vancouver, and we decided to attend. There was a seminar on house churches and Syl chose to attend. She was not very open to the idea that we were already a church. When she found me after the seminar, her first words were, "We are a church." Apparently the guy had a check list of things house churches do and we were doing all of them.

All this to say, we did not decide to plant a church, as most people do. We grew into a community of believers and non-believers on a journey together, trying to figure out how to walk with Jesus in this messed-up world. This Jesus thing can be very subversive.

The Theology ...

I believe the Bible to be the Word of God. I do not doubt its authenticity. I do however, question our interpretation of it.

The evolution in my theology only began as I stepped outside of the church in a real way to build relationships in the unchurched world. As I made friends and shared life, I realized that the theology I had been taught made me uncomfortable. It did not make sense outside of the church walls.

As I took a hard look at the life of Jesus, I realized that he did not, and could not, play by the rules we had set up as "The Church." Jesus wasn't a "peace at all costs" kind of guy. He wasn't as concerned about our comfort as we are. Jesus didn't just give a yearly offering to "the poor"; they were his friends. He liked all the people we looked down on. He hung out with criminals and hookers and tax collectors and poor people. In "the Church" our reason for being seemed to be to protect ourselves from the world Jesus lived in.

As we made attempts at integrating our friends into the existing church, we realized that at the end of the day, they did not understand this subculture we were involved in. Most of the time we walked away embarrassed, and our friends were confused. The problem was that the church didn't reflect us or the God we shared with our friends. It simply was not welcoming or hospitable to those who didn't fit the culture. They felt judged and they felt shunned.

We slowly became more comfortable with our unchurched friends than we did with church people. The world had valid questions, and the Church had very few acceptable answers, and was unwilling to admit the grey areas existed. We are all confused by some of what God says and does. The fact of the matter is, we do not have all the answers. God is bigger than our theologies. I do not even like some of what God says, but He is God. I have to walk in faith sometimes, and I hate it. But I love God, and I am learning to trust Him.

My view of what Church "is" was changed as we started to become a community. I began to notice that our community looked a whole lot more like the stuff Paul spoke of regarding the Church than did our local church on the corner. We knew each other; we ate together; we were in each other's lives. Issues like discipline became easier to manage because we were friends and reconciliation was the goal, not protecting ourselves from the blemish of sin (Remember Dallas Willard's "Gospel of sin management?")

As we learned to journey with each other and with God, we realized that our view of salvation was messed up. We were called to make disciples, not save people. Making disciples takes a long time. It is an investment. We had to start seeing people as God saw them. We needed to see them as dearly loved by God; His creation. So we needed to "let them in." We realized that people needed to belong, so that they could believe. This may not be the case for everyone, but it seems to be the way it is for many of those we have met. So now we have a guy who has done way too many drugs, sleeping them off on our sofa during a Sunday night open house. We learn to deal with a guy who drinks too much at our gatherings, and teach him how to drink responsibly and follow Jesus. It is messy, but it is real, and lives are changing.

Non-Negotiables

I don't argue theology anymore. I am interested in deep-water issues. What are my non-negotiables?

Jesus. To be a follower of Jesus, you need to be following, no matter how slowly. What did Jesus say and what did He do? Am I following in these things? Jesus cared about the poor a whole lot more than most Christians would like to admit. He made taking care of the poor a major criteria for salvation, and the only criterion for judgment

(Matthew 25). I had never been taught this at any church I attended. It was always about looking good and holy on Sunday, keeping up the appearance of perfection. I had to come to grips with, "Does Jesus inhabit my being, or does Church?"

In many ways the Bible is a much harder book than we have made it out to be, and at the same time, much simpler as well. It isn't rocket science. I think we have made it more complicated, so that we would not have to deal with its difficulty.

The Open Door has been functioning officially for 4 years. We average about 30 at our celebration at the moment; however, we have another 12 to 15 hardcore kids who do a study with me on Monday nights. They even find The Open Door daunting.

There are also those who are on the periphery of our community, those who are trying to figure out life and faith. They seem to want to be close, but not personal. Altogether there are probably between 75 and 100 people connected to our community. There are many who think we are a young people's church, because of who I am and the activities we embrace; however, we have quite a wide age range, much like typical church demographics. We have a lot of people in their 20s and 30s, and we also have people from 50 to 80. Bill and Bessie are in their late 70s or early 80s. They say they come to TOD because the Spirit of God's peace is here. We have had several weddings in the past four years, and so as a result little children are becoming more numerous.

People who may feel marginalized in an average evangelical church find their way to TOD as well. We have a few mentally ill people and a few alcoholics in our community. Everyone is welcome. Victor is a man in his 60s. He is an alcoholic and has no desire to stop drinking. He also loves Jesus. Sometimes Victor is more like Jesus than most people I know. He is always helping and taking care of others. There is no job too menial for Victor. He is a part of our community.

When we decided to have a corporate meeting at The Vault (our drop-in center), we had to decide what made sense in terms of activity. What do we do at this meeting? We chose to do three things. The first was to eat together. This is very important to us. Eating helps create community. The sharing of food is universal. No matter what background or culture you come from, food is a shared experience. I would argue that this is the most important aspect of our celebration. We have a community pot. Every week someone agrees to bring food for the next week. Whoever takes the pot, brings it back full the next week, and that is what we share. Soup, chili, salads, and barbecues in the summer are our favourites.

We are a community that is very musical. We have a very rock'n'roll heritage and many who appreciate the hardcore scene. I believe that worship needs to be indigenous, to come from within the community. To this end, a worship music experience was a need for us. So we have a time of worship which looks a lot like a concert. It is very chaordic. To a visitor, it may seem totally disorganized.

We have several very good musicians, but they are musicians at heart. We have an open mic, which allows anyone who wants to, to join the band on any given song. Sometimes, that means an amazing harmony happens, other times it means the sound man has to turn the mic off. It allows kids, mentally challenged people, amazing singers and tone-deaf people all to feel a part of the worship. Sam can get up to the mic with his hoodie up and do his best hip hop moves without ever singing a word, but he is in the moment and it is meaningful. Some days it is pretty ordinary: the band leads and nothing crazy happens, but we worship.

The third component is "teaching". My personal view is that teaching comes from within the community. We all learn from each other. We all have stuff to learn and teach. This time is more of an open forum facilitated by the person up front. Sometimes it looks like a semi-normal teaching session, only with heckling. Other times it can turn into a full-on argument, and it looks like the wheels are coming off.

I pay attention to the ebb and flow of our community. What are people dealing with? What are our struggles? How are we relating to each other and the world around us? Are there issues of faith that we need to address? Jesus is a big deal. How do we walk in this world and walk with Jesus at the same time? What does it mean to follow Jesus? In the past year we have been focusing on the words of Jesus, trying to understand what was important to him.

On paper, our gathering can look a lot like a "typical" church gathering; however, most people find the experience quite different. We are not seeking to be emerging, or postmodern, or post-post-modern. We are striving to be real and live out our life with Jesus in a way that touches our world and changes lives.

Leaders and Servants

Leadership is a hot button issue today in Church development. I am pretty sure God is more interested in servanthood. I am definitely the leader in our community, but I am a part of the community. This is my family, and we are friends.

Decisions within our community are made by people in the community. We have an informal structure for the most part, where whoever is in the room at the time of a decision has a say. Anyone can have a say. Even our neighbor, who is not "interested" at all in faith, has given input on some church decisions, because she was there and we asked what she would do. My kids, who are 16, 14, and 11, have had input into decisions, because they are a part of the community and may see things from a different perspective. We learn from each other. On rare occasions, someone has to have the final say. In those instances it would be in my lap, but these are rare cases.

Financial decisions are made by a semi-formal committee, because we are a part of the Free Methodist Church in Canada. However, the three members of this committee are a part of the community and therefore understand the heart of the community.

When you put a group of people in a room with no leadership structure and assign a task, in most cases, a structure will be created naturally. If the task is technical, then technical people will have the reins. If the task is financial, then the bankers will rise to the occasion. This is what happens in community. You learn what gifts and talents people bring to the table, and when the need arises, you let them run with it. This way, people feel appreciated and a genuine part of the community. I have very little understanding of finances. Show me a spreadsheet, and I will slip into a coma. I don't get it. So when it comes to that stuff, my wife and others run the show. I ask questions and trust my family members to manage the rest. I am the same way with computer technology.

In my opinion, leadership comes down to trust. If we can trust each other, then I don't have to control everything (Think, "The Speed of Trust.")

When we were trying to figure this whole church thing out, I was approached by Jared Siebert, who at the time was a pastor at Next in Kingston, about becoming part of FMC. I later met with Dan Sheffield and explained that I needed three things from FMC. First, I needed to be involved with a community of similar church leaders who understood where I was coming from. Second, I needed money. Third, I wanted to be left alone to do what God was calling us to. I did not want a denomination to try to control something they didn't understand. All three of my conditions were accepted. So far, I am thrilled with the community and the hands-off aspects of our arrangement. The financial part has been a struggle, due to available funding; however, FMC is doing what it can, and we continue to trust God for the rest. We are blessed to be able to do what we feel God has called us to.

The Future in the Past

Most of my mentors are dead, or they are movie characters. My father-in-law, Joe Kass, is definitely up there. He is 72, and never stops learning. He has watched our community grow with some skepticism, and has become a full-on part of it. He continues to live life to the fullest, while dealing with a cancer that should have claimed him two years ago. He trusts God and loves life. He is a grandfather to my kids and our community. When he was skeptical, he watched without criticism. When he saw the fruit, he rejoiced rather than rationalize.

I love John Wesley, but I recognize that he was not Jesus. He was as messed up as the rest of us, but he was relentless in his passion for God and the poor.

C.S. Lewis was a genius. He was postmodern long before the word was invented. If half the people who idolized him actually understood his writing, they would call him a heretic.

John McLane, was a solution-oriented, passionate man, who was willing to do whatever it took to get the job done and save those he loved.

175

John Constantine and William Wallace are up there as well.

I guess the bottom line for me is that planting churches may be the wrong goal: building community is the place to start. Many church plants fail, due to disagreements, vision, etc. Most church planters recruit a core group. However, if these people are not invested in each other, if they don't become family, then when times get tough, when differences occur, people leave. In building community, we build lasting relationships. It isn't always pretty; more often than not it is messy, but it is real. "Church" should not be about worship style, targeting people groups, or any of those things. It should be about walking together, celebrating God in our lives and loving our neighbors.

I have been asked many times how we do what we do at The Open Door. I can tell people what we do, but I cannot provide a formula to be copied; neither can anyone else. Every community is different. We have different needs, personalities, neighbors and contexts. Trying to duplicate a system for what a church is supposed to be, doesn't work. In this sense, community grows out of the context of the mission, and I think our record proves that. We will continue to be and build community, learning what it means to follow Jesus and love this world that God created, together.

About Kim Reid

Kim Reid (Montreal, QC) has been involved in youth work and ministry for 30 years. In 1992, while working professionally with emotionally disturbed adolescents, he began The Vault, a drop-in center for teens, under Youth For Christ. In 1996 he started On Rock Ministries, under whose umbrella The Vault continued to grow and thrive. On Rock expanded into community services, such as a food bank and a lunch program for under-privileged elementary school kids. Kim and Sylvia have been married for 26 years and have three amazing children.

Chapter 12

theStory, Sarnia
Nathan Colquhoun

theStory is a church community in Sarnia, Ontario, started in 2006. It was planted by Darryl Silvestri, Joe Manafo and me, each of us with a similar desire to experiment with something new. At the time, while attending Tyndale University College in Toronto, I could not find a single church that made sense to me. I'm not sure what kind of church I was looking for, or why I thought I would have any better luck at starting something, but the combination of this fruitless search for a church and a growing desire to live in community was enough to put me on a path back to my hometown of Sarnia to put the feelings I had into play.

For a long time I've been called a church planter but I don't like to call myself that anymore. Not only is theStory not a church plant any longer, but I also haven't planted any other churches. I didn't plant theStory by myself. Most of the people who are part of us now are not there because of me. My part in theStory no longer has anything to do with planting, and I've never really seen church planting as a career. Church planting was never something I needed to sustain me and to pay my bills, and it's not a great career path if you plan on making a living.

Planting a church was a natural step in my life, but not something I sought out or had in mind as a life goal. I didn't even know there was such a thing until I attended a conference in Toronto on the subject. Prior to the conference I was just interested in starting a church in Sarnia, and was unaware of the language and subculture that seems to have grown up around the practice. So, uninformed on more than one occasion, our journey with theStory has been one of genuine false starts and accidental successes. Perhaps if we had been exposed to the industry and culture of church planting things would have turned out differently, but maybe not for the better.

I've learned a few things over the last seven years, and share my experiences in the following paragraphs. I hope that they are of help to you in your own endeavors.

Community

Planting the church as a team (and not just with our wives) allowed us to be weak without having to hide it. It allowed us to bring balance to each other in ways that many leaders do not intend. It humbled us. It gave us support when we needed it the most. So as things began to evolve the team changed, but it never resolved to one person trying to navigate the ship. Solitude in leadership is hazardous. It creates monsters who are unable to be in relationships unless they are getting their own way, or it makes depression a constant threat. Either way, I've learned that it's healthier to plant as a team.

Near the beginning of theStory, I was just starting to appreciate the theology of community in terms of doing life together. Life together in the new monastic commune/Shane Clairborne kind of life that I learned about through college interested me more and more. It was hard to explain this to my wife. I wanted to (and I still do) live with other people that I am not related to by blood. I am considered by most friends to have what they call FOMO: Fear Of Missing Out. I land 100 percent extroverted on all the tests, and I see relationships as central to my life. theStory would have failed multiple times over if any of us would have attempted this alone. My understanding of Christian faith and the role of the Church in the world is summed up in small communities living, eating, and serving together. So I pressure and pressure again people from theStory to try and imagine their lives so intricately intertwined with others.

Needless to say, it never really worked. It was easy convincing the single men to move into the house with us and care about doing life together. The same ones have been there for three years and it really is a beautiful arrangement. A few other families who ironically no longer are part of theStory continue to live on the same block as us. So while there are small pockets of hope, things are still a long way off from my utopia.

All this longing for community becomes tiresome when there is so little fulfillment; so eventually I've had to adopt different, synchronous levels of community. There is the community you live with, the community you are neighbours with, the community you worship with, the community you play sports with, the community you party with, the community you learn and study with, and the community you serve with. It's too compartmentalized for my liking, but it's my only option at this time. I had to stop putting my expectations of community onto the community I worship with. I had to separate my longing to see families of Christians move into low-income neighbourhoods from my expectations of theStory. Maybe, one day, that will change.

Despite these lessons, community still stands as central to anything I have ever learned about church planting. It is the primary reason I moved back to Sarnia, it is the reason I am staying here, and it is the reason I have these kinds of reasons. A day after I received the keys to my house, twenty people from theStory showed up to help renovate. Earlier that same day, we met to worship and eat together as part of our Sunday gathering. You can't buy that kind of commitment. Watching your friends' children perform their ballet recital in their living room and then going on vacation with them isn't an average experience. You can't fabricate those kinds of friendships, or create them overnight. I'm hooked on these experiences, and I'm learning to help cultivate these expressions of church community without forcing them on others.

Kingdom

In 2004, my New Testament professor asked our classroom what Jesus was all about. We all put up our hands and gave him our Sunday school answers: "To save us from our sins! To show us a better way to live! To show us what love looked like! To be a living sacrifice!" We had so many

179

great answers, but he said they were all incomplete. I've spent the rest of my life exploring what the professor taught us that day: Jesus is all about the Kingdom of God.

There was a reason Jesus told parables to explain the Kingdom of God. It isn't something that you can define in a dictionary, but something that must be lived and experienced. So words don't do it justice. Stories help bring a bit more clarity. The Kingdom of God is like a seed, a net, a found treasure, and leaven. Our understanding of who we are and where we are going all hinges on this phrase, 'Kingdom of God.' The longer I stick at this, the more right it feels and the more excited I get about it and the deeper I want to go.

The Kingdom of God is like a church plant, full of joy and sorrow, and constantly forces one to re-evaluate his or her decisions and life. The Kingdom of God is like someone who has never been to church before finding safety within our church community. The Kingdom of God is like children having healthy role models and families eating together. The Kingdom of God is like hearing someone's story of abuse turn into a story of health and love. The Kingdom of God is like people being honest about their misgivings and boasting in their weakness. The Kingdom of God is like seeing the look on a single mom's face when she comes up from the water after being baptized. The Kingdom of God is like giving someone a reason not to hate God, and instead see good in the world and understand that they are loved. The Kingdom of God is like seeing middle-class families take families in poverty under their wings and bend over backwards to love and serve them. The Kingdom of God is like someone finding worth and purpose. The Kingdom of God is like starting a church from an idea and seeing it grow into a living thing, a community full of life.

Money

You can't serve God and Money. That's one of the most straightforward statements Jesus could have made. So I'm not sure why churches who are supposed to serve God have such horrendous views and practices around finances; wherever you look there is money corrupting churches, families and individuals. theStory isn't really all that special when it comes to money. We have a budget, we have had paid pastors, we pay for our building and we have a really small budget to help other people when they need it. Sure, we don't coerce people into giving their hard-earned paycheques to parking lot funds? We don't even take up a collection. There is just a tin can sitting at the front of the building that gives people the opportunity to support the church. Outside of that we are not anything special.

One of the ways that we were able to continue planting a church the way we have was that I started a business the same year we started the church. So I would make websites, take pictures, run sound equipment, organize events and do pretty much what anyone would pay me to do to pay my bills and not need to be supported by the church community. It worked even better after a year or so because theStory purchased a building in downtown Sarnia, so I was able to work from the building when I needed to be in the office, and represent theStory and its interests during the week.

Over time, I started fantasizing about what it would look like to have a business that acted like a business and made money and was able to sustain the church community. This would mean covering the rent for the building, employing pastors or subsidizing them, being present in the community in which the building was located and worrying about all the money parts of the relationship. One of the main reasons I loved this model was because it separated the two masters with which churches wrestle. If the church no longer had to deal with or constantly pursue money then it might be a healthier expression of life. We are moving further along with this idea now. The business has taken on a new life and is incorporated. I am one of five owners and there are eight people who work for the company. Five of us have some kind of leadership role at theStory.

It's not a perfect model by any means. Two of the guys in the company are self-proclaimed atheists and don't care much about the ins and outs of the work of the church. The business decisions of the company directly affect the reputation of the church. Many times people have a hard time seeing any difference, any separation between the two. It's complicated, so we are still working out this practice. What we have discovered is that money is difficult and a snare, so it's necessary for churches to take drastic measures to deal with a disease that is so common and so integrated into daily living.

181

Teaching

If there is one thing we do well at theStory, it is our teaching. We have a number of people who are Bible college- or seminary-educated, and who have at least attempted to read N.T. Wright's literary onslaught. We now have seven or so people who take turns teaching on a Sunday morning. We've spent eight months in Genesis, eight months in the parables, eight months in the gospel of John, a few months in Ephesians, Colossians and Philippians. We end up buying eight to ten books and commentaries on the text, and then devour them as we go through the series. It's a lot of fun. It's like sitting in school again at times when I'm preparing my sermons and seeing all the different arguments and views on passages and stories.

We also have discussion during our teaching times. We have ten rules of dialogue that frame and help guide the discussion in an attempt to make it fruitful and edifying. We don't podcast or put anything online as we think that if you want just the information you can read the books we read. We've never really made it easy for people to be part of our community without actually being part of our community. Teaching for us is far from a show: it's community time where we attempt to take everyone from all these different walks of life and shape them in the same understanding of who we are, who God is, and what it's like to be part of God's Kingdom.

This struggle to strip away all the public sides of our teaching revealed a lot about the role that preaching had taken in most of our lives. Many of us could listen to a sermon online and feel like we were "fed" and go without worshiping in community for months. Others could listen to sermons and not make the connection to living. Our lives are so compartmentalized that we can talk about serving the poor every Sunday for a year and not see any significant increase in folks doing it. When it's just sixty people in a room talking it out and allowing God's story to seep into their lives, these realities of intellectualization become a lot more obvious. Sometimes the teacher is verbally challenged by listeners. Sometimes the question is posed like, "Why do we justify ourselves out of anything that demands sacrifice?" It took stripping it down to the bare minimum and looking people in the eye to recognize our own brokenness. Only the repeated act of breaking bread together, humbly confessing our inability to change, and worshiping together was going to have any effect on us as a community. So while our preaching is good, we are starting to realize that it doesn't really impact us as much as we had once believed.

Staying

One of the ongoing jokes we have with our out-of-town friends is constantly asking them when they are going to move to Sarnia. Sometimes it actually works, and they pick up their lives and move! You can catch us reminiscing about our lives on summer evenings, smelling the beach air, sitting on a back porch admiring how rich our lives are. We really do at times feel like we have it all, and all we want to do is share it with everyone else, especially those who aren't finding contentment in their current situation. So we've moved a number of people here and integrated them into our community. Some have stayed and others have left.

There is a certain amount of fear nowadays about commitment. Not so much a commitment to a person, but a commitment to a place. In a culture of privilege, it is seen as moving downward to choose to stay. We are convinced that choosing to stay means choosing not to embark on all the new things that God might have in store for you: things that would require not staying and thus missing out on so much that life offers here and now. Choosing to stay means that you are saying no to leaving, so most people never actually choose to be where they are. They want to leave their options open. It reminds me of the David Bazan song when he lets us in on a conversation where the man says to the woman, "I could never divorce you / Without a good reason / And though I may never have to / It's good to have options." But healthy relationships are built on stability and trust. It's hard to have a healthy relationship with a people and a place if you aren't committed to them.

Staying let's people around us know we are serious. It allows people to grow in trust. You stay with what you love. If you keep wondering if someone is going to show up or if they are going to take a job elsewhere or if they are just going to get bored, it changes the way the present feels and can be lived out. What I can gather from people who have gone before me is that there is value in staying put, sinking roots in and refusing to leave, even when there are hardships. Communities grow in depth and season in richness like fine wine, same as in a marriage.

Leadership

I left leadership until last because it is has been one of the most challenging practices at theStory. Personally I've toyed with ideas from a Papist model to Christo-anarchism. I still have very little idea what is right—or at least right for us. In a Canadian context there are good arguments for all sorts of models, and all of them have their own strengths and weaknesses.

The first I mentioned earlier: planting in team. Balancing power, responsibility and sharing the load, for us, has been a healthy choice. I see only problems with a model that puts one person in power while simultaneously placing the burden of pastoring a church solely on them. When you have two or more people who take on those responsibilities, then the weight of leadership is shared amongst them. Their roles may vary depending on gifts and needs, but they mutually submit to each other as they help shape the direction and rhythm of the church. For theStory, this has been a crucial move. If "power corrupts, and absolute power corrupts absolutely," then why give power or control or full responsibility to one person?

Secondly, the way leaders recognize themselves in relation to others directly affects their ability to lead well. If leaders are not humble and self-aware there is a danger of being passive-aggressive as a means of controlling others, exposing themselves to depression if things don't go their way, or having to constantly remind people of their authority. Leaders must be servants. Any other 'title' given or received (i.e., cultural architect, teaching pastor, narrator, creative director, senior pastor) will only serve to confuse their primary goal as servants. It's not that these titles are unfit, but that they tend to attribute power rather than responsibility. Servanthood should be the character of all responsibility.

Third, there should be no distinction between paid leaders and unpaid leaders. Money should never be a deciding factor in someone's role or title. This is something very difficult to practice, and we've never really done it well, because money is a great motivator. By giving only those who are paid certain responsibilities, especially important ones, you begin to create a culture where money motivates living the faith. You eventually then have churches where pastors are paid to be professional

Christians and everyone else is expected to be good people and give money: a class system, or a new kind of priesthood.

Alternatively, it's healthy to share authority and responsibility more broadly, including people who are not paid. This isn't to discard the idea of paying pastors, but a corrective to the way money divides believers into classes. We pay pastors because we want to free them up to do something that someone else can't, not because it's a career or profession.

Again, these are just lessons I've learned along the way about leadership. Every community is a complex organism that needs folks to constantly be humbling themselves and listening to each other so that they grow healthy and strong. For the same model to be applied to every community is oppressive and unwise.

Conclusion

Church planting is not a skill. The best church planter I know spent his first year sweeping the front steps of a building he bought, runs multiple meat bingos every month, and runs a thrift store in the church basement. This church planter did not read a book or take a class on church planting. He didn't read this book. He just moved into a neighbourhood and loved it. This is what church planting is. It's choosing to be God's representatives in places that have been abandoned and forgotten. It's choosing to bring peace where there is strife, and bring love where there is chaos, and commitment where there is none.

The points I've highlighted are not a step-by-step way to plant a successful church; they are lessons that I have learned in trying to live the Kingdom way in Sarnia, Ontario. The reality is that we don't plant churches at all: we live somewhere, try to discover what God is up to, and then join in his work. We participate in the redemption and reconciliation of all things within a local context. We can call this church planting, but really it is us allowing God to shape and form us into his people.

So I hope our story inspires you, warns you, and directs you. I hope the lessons I've learned shed wisdom, and, above all, I hope that you and your church are being shaped not by formulas and expectations, but by the gentle graceful hand of our Creator.

About Nathan Colquhoun

Nathan Colquhoun is a director of Storyboard Solutions, pastor at theStory, lover of Rachel, citizen of Sarnia, and neighbour on College Ave S. He blogs at nathancolquhoun.com.

Chapter 13

Church Planting in the City
Sean Benesh

Sunday afternoons for my family are designated times for the "switchbacks sessions." You see, my older two sons are longboarders and every Sunday afternoon a group of riders gather together at the "switchbacks" at the bottom of Washington Park here in Portland to ride. Anywhere from twenty to forty riders show up to shred with other local greats, or learn how to fine-tune their craft whether cornering, tucking, or simply free-riding. At times part of the group breaks off, jumps on the MAX light rail, takes it to the top of the west ridge, and rides the infamous ZooBomb back down. Most Sundays I usually drop the boys off at the switchbacks and walk over to one of the coffee shops in the Goose Hollow neighborhood.

Goose Hollow is one of my favorite neighborhoods in all of Portland; in many ways it is an anomaly. When most people reference this neighborhood they either talk about Washington Park, with its well-known rose gardens and Japanese garden, or Jeld-Wen Field where Portland's MLS club, the Timbers, play. The MAX light rail line weaves its way through the neighborhood bringing people in from all parts of the city to watch a Timbers game. But surprisingly, Goose Hollow is one of the more high-density neighborhoods in Portland as it sits on the western flank of downtown Portland separated only by a freeway. In fact, it is perfectly hemmed in by freeways on two sides, Washington Park on the west, and Burnside Road on the north.

As I walk down the massive hills in Goose Hollow towards the coffee shop I find myself counting the leveled stories of apartment buildings and condos. I notice quite a number of pedestrians, especially when I walk along the MAX line close to the stadium. The neighborhood has a very activating feel about it. After I arrive in the coffee shop I sit by the big windows where I can take note of the "sidewalk ballet"[1] that is taking place outside. This urban neighborhood has over 6,000 residents within its rather small boundaries, and yet there is no church planting taking place. Why?

It was these kinds of dynamics and questions that sent me on an expedition about five years ago to figure out why church planting in urban neighborhoods was lagging behind other places like the suburban fringe. I conducted research, interviews, and surveys as part of my dissertation at Bakke Graduate University which turned into the book *Metrospiritual: The Geography of Church Planting*. I continue to revisit this topic. But each time I do, I'm prompted to ask: Has anything changed in the geography of church planting over the last five years?

In the course of writing this chapter today I had coffee with one of my former seminary students who took a church planting course I gave. One of the textbooks for the class was *Metrospiritual*. I commented to him that in some ways the book was growing obsolete. If I were to start all over in my research of the site selection for new church plants, what would I find? In this chapter I will revisit some of those initial assumptions and questions in light of the current cultural milieu around urban church planting.

The quest to discover the geographic placement of new churches took root during the time I served as a church planting strategist in Tucson, Arizona. About a year into my new role I spent time with a number of church planters, as well as prospective church planters who came to Tucson to explore the possibility of planting a church with us. I slowly began to see a trend, to which I paid more attention throughout the following year, leading to new convictions as my ministry began to unfold.

I vividly remember the day it hit me because I wrote a blogpost titled "Jesus Loves White Affluent Suburbanites," on my blog at theurbanloft.org. At that point I probably worked with 50 potential and actual church planters. Without actual documentation, I would venture to say that roughly 80 to 90 percent of them "felt called" to plant churches in the suburbs. I cynically thought to myself, "If God is calling all of these church planters to the suburbs then he must not like ethnic urbanites because he's not calling anyone there." Afterwards, I began doing informal surveys in other cities and the results looked the same over and over again. Thus, my quest began.[2]

Fast forward the story to today and I have lived in two cities in the Pacific Northwest: Vancouver, BC in Canada, and Portland, Oregon. I have had the opportunity to observe the geographic placement of new churches in these two cities, both of which were part of my dissertation research. Not only that, but I have spent considerably more time reading and researching on urban geography, and looking at related topics like site selection or geographic placement of new businesses or sports stadiums. From my fresh vantage point here in inner-city Portland I have watched the trends and the tide change for church plants. Today, urban is cool and chic.

My initial question from *Metrospiritual* is still valid. "Why do all of the hip and trendy neighborhoods, whether urban gentrified or suburban, get a plethora of church planters while less desirable parts of the city get little to none?"[3] On a weekly basis I spend a lot of time in coffee shops in various urban neighborhoods throughout inner-city Portland. Often times I run into church planters and pastors in these settings. There are times when I have looked up from my laptop to spot two to three (or more) church planters in the same place, not sure if they are aware of one another. Why are there so many planters in one part of the city? I acknowledge by my presence that I am part of the equation. Guilty as charged. What woos me to urban neighborhoods are also the same influences, factors and changing cultural dynamics that are reorienting cities globally.

Last month I led a workshop called the "Gentrification Primer" where I taught on the dynamics and process of gentrification, not just in Portland, but in cities across the country and globe. One of those "A-HA!" moments came when we collectively walked through the changing dynamics reshaping American cities in particular. Whereas cities once expanded outward sending people like a giant centrifuge to the suburbs, much has changed and the pull now is more centripetal. That does not mean that cities are not growing outward and expanding, but because of larger cultural influences more people are forgoing the suburbs and the "American Dream" to move back into the core. As I wrote in my book *The Multi-Nucleated Church*, Americans are growing in their desire for an urban lifestyle.[4] Nona Aronowitz comments, "Six in 10 people also said they would sacrifice a bigger house to live in a neighborhood that featured a mix of houses, stores, and businesses within an easy walk."[5]

That night at the workshop I saw a healthy mixture representing the changes that gentrification in a neighborhood is forging. On one hand there were longstanding residents (African-American) who lived in the same neighborhood for the past 40 years watching their neighborhood change. On the other there were young, educated, middle-class whites who moved into the city center precisely because of the appeal of an urban lifestyle. This same appeal has brought more people into the core and church planters are following on their heels. In many ways this is good missiology, as church planters tend to be pretty adept at reading cultural trends and fads. But that does not resolve the tension that church planters and their supporters favor sexy cities and appealing, livable, up-and-coming neighborhoods whether urban or suburban. "It is easy to love a city and parts of the city that are beautiful, well-maintained, and safe. When cities are undesirable, dangerous, and wild our love is truly tested."[6]

These changes mean more than simply a reshuffling of people has occurred. New people move in and existing residents are priced out, having to move further out and away from essential services. As more investment takes place in city centers and the central business district, it has driven structural and economic changes also. Many cities are scrambling to retrofit their urban areas, whether with such things as light rail, streetcars, or an expanded bicycling infrastructure. New districts of consumption are being created as people consume the urban lifestyle.[7] This means more conversion of older buildings into residential apartment lofts and condos or new build-from-scratch high-density urban neighborhoods like False Creek in Vancouver, or South Waterfront in Portland.

Economically, agglomeration economies mean that place and site selection for businesses are more important than ever before. "The benefits of clustering are well known: firms benefit from knowledge transfer, the availability of shared resources, better access to workers, suppliers and customers, and value added by the reputation of their location. These advantages seem to have endured despite claims that new technologies have rendered spatial proximity less relevant for contemporary firms."[8] Many of these clustering dynamics are taking place in city centers, especially in the burgeoning artisan economy. "Clusters of creative and cultural industries are said to flourish where there are strong networks and pivotal institutions."[9]

So what are the implications for church planting in urban contexts? The changes and dynamics at hand are massively reorienting cities culturally, structurally, socially, and economically. I have observed these changes take place over the course of my research and writing of Metrospiritual and then subsequently. What we also fail to grasp is the spiritual make-up of cities. Jacques Ellul notes, "The city has, then, a spiritual influence. It is capable of directing and changing a man's [sic] spiritual life. It brings its power to bear in him and changes his life, all his life, not just his house."[10]

There are so many layers to the city, and urban church planters must be cognizant of them. On one hand they may be dealing with social issues that are the result of a neighborhood shake-up due to gentrification. Often what is really at play is an economic conversation, and in some case bullying and corruption where developers and investors seek to "flip" neighborhoods for a profit. At the heart of that profiteering is sin. As a result, the conversation on development and gentrification is a spiritual conversation.

For this reason, church planters moving into urban neighborhoods need to be aware of these changes and plant churches that are sensitive to context. "The forces shaping cities play an enormous role in the geography of church planting. The decision of where to [plant] is critical to the future trajectory of the church because the setting or context influences so much."[11] What is needed in contextualized urban church planting is a new set of skills, rhythms, and postures adopted by a new generation of church planters. I have broken this down into two distinct categories: place-based postures, and missionary skills

Place-Based Postures

Jon Huckins in his book *Thin Places* writes about the postures that he and his community in the Golden Hills neighborhood of San Diego have adopted. This community of Jesus followers in this urban neighborhood sees itself as missionaries or "sent ones." They covenant together to dwell in a similar way that Jesus demonstrated in the Incarnation. "God is so passionate about missionally extending into the human neighborhood that he moves into it."[12] As a community imbedded in and part of the neighborhood fabric, they committed to one another to do such things as live within a ten-minute walking distance from each other, regularly share common meals, regularly gather for worship, live in mission together, and participate in the neighborhood.[13]

As a covenant community of missionaries in their neighborhood, they have a place-based framework from which they operate. Through much time, prayer, conversation and discernment, this community, and many like it in their network, has adopted a rule or *regula*: a set of regular practices. In the challenge of urban church planting, these postures are invaluable and life-giving.

- *Listening:* We desire to be attuned to God, to self, and to our neighborhood.
- *Submerging:* We desire to embody Jesus in our neighborhood while participating in an apprenticing community.
- *Inviting:* We desire to grasp the depth of God's invitation to Kingdom life, and to become more inviting and invited people while welcoming our neighbors into God's redemptive story.
- *Contending:* We desire to confront the things that hinder the full expression of the Kingdom of God, both spiritual and natural, in our community, among our friends and neighbors, and in our city.
- *Imagining:* We desire to discern God's intent on our lives and help share transformational faith communities.
- *Entrusting:* We desire to entrust people to God and to others, celebrate our deeper understanding of God's call on our lives, and lean confidently into our future.[14]

These place-based postures continue to reframe how church planting can be done, especially in urban contexts where complexity reigns. This necessarily leads into the next category as we move from place-based postures to missionary skills. All this is critical in re-imagining church planting in urban contexts.

Missionary Skills

Tradecraft: For the Church on Mission, written by a team of seasoned missionary workers, is a book that offers to the public the "missionary skills" that are essential. Written like a spy manual, and like the name suggests, this is the "inside scoop" of what missionaries "over there" are to be about. The back cover of the book reads, "This book, in essence, pulls back the curtain on tools once accessible only to full-time Christian workers moving overseas, and offers them to anyone anywhere who desires to live missionally." The purpose of the book is to share these insights widely, because being a missionary is not about geography, but identity. All who are in Christ are living in the *missio Dei*. The skills explored in this book serve as a foundation for rich engagement for urban church planters.

- *Following the Spirit:* Rather than focus on being initially strategy-oriented, the first questions to ask are, "What does Scripture have to say on how we develop our mission strategy? Aren't we supposed to be following the Spirit?"[15]
- *Mapping:* This skill, utilizing Kevin Lynch's mapping model,[16] focuses on an intimate understanding of your neighborhood in knowing where the paths, nodes, edges, districts, and landmarks are. This better equips you to decide where and how to engage in mission.
- *Exegeting Culture:* Building off of mapping, "Cultural exegesis is a basic missionary skill that allows us to see a people's context through spiritual eyes that discern the bridges and barrier to the communication of the gospel."[17]
- *Building Relationships:* The foundation for missional engagement begins in the simple act of building relationships.
- Identifying Persons of Peace: The "person of peace" is the person who is a natural networker and leader in his or her social circles. It is essential for the gospel to move to identify this person who opens up the relational doors.
- *Engaging Tribes:* This skill entails noting and then identifying with a specific tribe, social grouping, or residents in a particular geographic locale.

- *Contextualization:* "Contextualization is the translation of the gospel from one culture to another."[18] Learning how to translate and communicate the gospel is an essential missionary skill. "The cultural soil dictates much of how churches are being planted, or at least it should."[19]
- *Pursuing Alternative Paths:* In the context of mission there are many avenues to live as "sent ones" which do not entail the traditional approach of occupational ministry. Oftentimes these alternative paths open the door for further ministry.
- *Protecting Indigeneity:* "When people must abandon their valued cultural identity and adopt an alien culture in order to become believers, the cause of church planting will not go far."[20]

Combined with the placed-based postures that Huckins offers, the missionary skills in *Tradecraft* move the conversation forward about what it means to be church planters (i.e., missionaries) in our home cities. These postures and skills are not simply for the "professional clergy," or for boards trying to put more seats in the pew, but for everyday followers of Jesus. There is much to learn from both books that applies to urban contexts, whether planting among the marginalized or the creative class.

What I learned through the process of researching and writing *Metrospiritual* is that a new approach is needed to proclaim and embody the gospel in urban neighborhoods, whether in North America or globally. A new approach gleans from what missionaries have learned "over there," combining that knowledge with a growing understanding of the dynamic that is shaping Western cities. It then applies that knowledge and opens it to church planters, missionaries, or sent ones "over here." That is the heart of what it means to be metrospiritual.

About Sean Benesh

Sean Benesh, DMin., has been involved in urban ministry in the capacity of adjunct professor, researcher, lecturer, consultant, church planter, and has also worked as a hiking and mountain biking guide in southern Arizona and an urban cycling guide in Portland, Oregon. He is the author of four books on urban ministry and is currently working on a number of upcoming books on the topics of gentrification, the urbanity of the Bible, theology of urban mission, and the intersection of missiology and urban form.

Bibliography

Aronowitz, Nona Willis. "Most Americans Want a Walkable Neighborhood, Not a Big House." *Good.* No pages. Online: http://www.good.is/posts/most-americans-want-a-walkable-neighborhood-not-a-big-house.

Benesh, Sean. *Metrospiritual: The Geography of Church Planting.* Eugene: Resource Publications, 2011.

_____. *The Multi-Nucleated Church: Towards a Theoretical Framework for Church Planting in High-Density Cities.* Portland: Urban Loft, 2012.

Ellul, Jacques. *The Meaning of the City.* Grand Rapids: William B. Eerdmans, 1970.

Huckins, Jon. *Thin Places: Six Postures for Creating and Practicing Missional Community.* Kansas City: The House Studio, 2012.

Jacobs, Jane. *The Death and Life of Great American Cities.* New York: Random House, 1961.

Lynch, Kevin. *The Image of the City.* Cambridge: The MIT Press, 1960.

McCrary, Larry, et al, *Tradecraft: For the Church on Mission.* Portland: Urban Loft, 2013.

Smith, Andrew. *Events and Urban Regeneration: The Strategic Use of Events to Revitalize Cities.* New York: Routledge, 2012.

---

1 Jane Jacobs uses this term in her book *The Death and Life of Great American Cities.*

2 Benesh, *Metrospiritual*, 5.

3 Ibid., 79.

4 Benesh, *The Multi-Nucleated Church*, 54.

5 Aronowitz, "Most Americans Want a Walkable Neighborhood, Not a Big House."

6 *Metrospiritual*, 153.

7 Places like The Pearl in Portland, and Yaletown in Vancouver are examples.

8 Smith, *Events and Urban Regeneration*, 173.

9 Ibid., 175.

10 Ellul, *The Meaning of the City*, 9.

11 *Metrospiritual*, 117.

12 Huckins, *Thin Places*, 19.

13 Ibid., 13.

14 Ibid., 28.

15 McCrary et al, *Tradecraft*, 38.

16 Lynch, *The Image of the City*.

17 *Tradecraft*, 73.

18 Ibid., 148.

19 *Metrospiritual*, 119.

20 *Tradecraft*, 187.

Chapter 14

Top Challenges for Missional Church Planting in Urban North America
Dan Steigerwald

For over two decades now, I've had the privilege of being involved in church planting and pioneering leadership (both directly and/or walking alongside as a coach to such leadership). Here's some of what I've seen as the greatest challenges to successful church planting, which I would venture to say may have relevance in any cultural setting. Two things I'll mention up front: 1) Spiritual warfare is not on the list below – it's just assumed at every level – and 2), the order below does not represent any ranking by importance, but simply my own outpouring of thoughts. I do invite feedback, as any list will inevitably leave out or inadequately represent challenges experienced by practitioners doing their best against many odds. I still use the word "planting" because it seems to have currency with an evangelical audience (though "birthing" is perhaps a more accurate term for describing the process of starting missional incarnational churches). For Presbyterians and other mainline groups, the phrase "new church development" (NCD) is used synonymously with "church planting."

Funding needs and limitations restrict the point leader(s)

I think if a leader is convinced God has called him/her to plant, he/she needs to go for it and not make funding the central go/no-go question. Too many leaders are hesitant to move forward at all without the guarantee of a solid funding trajectory. Still, the choice to plant demands resolute and creative attention to support-raising, both at the start of the project and throughout. Today's economic realities and the diminished availability of resources from individuals and sponsoring agencies mean that many planters need to work bi-vocationally.

This can present another major challenge in and of itself – having inadequate time left over to deliver the leadership energy and presence needed to birth a full-orbed missional church. Yes, I realize the advantage of bi-vocational planting for the sake of embedding and identifying with context and those we're placed among. This can be a very good strategy, especially if one's job is flexible and/or complementary to the church planting process. But I also recognize the idealism associated with insistence upon a bi-vocational stance (more often than not coming from first-time church planters). To corral and synergize the people and resources needed to plant a church that's attentive to new discipleship, equipping and multiplication requires leadership energy, time and presence in context (even more so in disadvantaged neighborhoods where radical brokenness and need are regularly encountered).

That's nearly impossible to deliver if one is tied up with more than a half-time job (especially as the project gains momentum). Notice I said "nearly impossible," meaning that it may be possible if there's enough leadership finesse, skill and experience within the team leader and his/her planting team (who also cannot be too bogged down with work commitments outside the project).

Lack of Team Diversity or Strength

How many times have we seen new seminary grads collectively decide they're going to plant, only to find that together they are too much alike in their shepherd-teaching orientations (wired primarily to cultivate nurturing and edification of the forming, local body of Christ)? A high density of such role propensities makes it hard for planting teams to model and embed the outward missional DNA, which actually needs to be over-accented in the early phases of planting. Other leader-types of the apostolic, prophetic and evangelistic variety are needed to counterbalance the inward community-building dynamic. (By the way, I think this outward "sodalic" energy needs to be continually fueled and cultivated throughout the full life-cycle of a church, given the centripetal – toward-the-center – force that bodies of Christians quickly generate when they taste authentic community together).

In addition to preserving the inward/outward tension on a leadership team, I'm also a firm believer that certain core leadership competencies must be present in a team leader (or spread among a leadership team – not to the exclusion of a designated point leader, mind you. In my experience, and the data seems to back this up, few teams operate effectively without a "lead orchestrator"). The reality is that it is hard to move groups of people forward without certain basic leadership aptitude and skills (e.g. strategy, pioneering, visioning, communication, basic team-equipping skills, etc.). It is not enough to simply rally and cohere a group of Christians together and call this a church plant. Planting teams need to generate momentum, outwardly and inwardly, so that people are equipped to live a Jesus way of life that both demonstrates the good news and also provokes new discipleship. Now, having made the plug for robust, diverse leadership, I do think that planting teams deficient in leader strength or diversity should not be dissuaded from initiating the planting process. If they are willing to learn some needed skills along the way, while also creating a berth for additional leader(s) to eventually emerge or join them, they may well be able to get a new church up and running.

Team Implosion

This used to be the single greatest factor that crashed plants, and I'd venture to say it probably still is at the top. Whoever is running on point, regardless of how shared the leadership function is, he/she better be committed not only to equipping their core team and stakeholders but also to developing and holistically forming their emerging leaders. This means those called to lead and steward and serve a forming community better prioritize and demonstrate their own commitment to personal development; otherwise, the whole team development process, no matter how well-intended, will eventually falter.

Of course, there's also no substitute for understanding team formation dynamics. And plant teams that want to grow and work effectively will need to take the time to understand mutual giftedness, passions, personality, etc., of each team member, including normal formative cycles of teams over time. It's important to add that building an environment of trust, respect and mutuality may well posture an average team to accomplish far more than a highly-gifted team not cultivating their capacity to work well together.

"Over-Missioning" at the Expense of a More Holistic Discipleship Stance

A good number of planting teams adopt social justice and compassion impact as the measures of success, rather than broad-based impact across a bigger swath than marginalized populations or a single neighborhood or population group. New discipleship out of the sphere of natural relationships often plays second fiddle to the ideal of making a visible difference in righting societal wrongs and spheres of neglect and oppression along a certain narrow band. These are definitely important foci for planting teams, but missional communities must project themselves beyond the rescue, solve-the-problem motif. Jesus is the Savior and Rejuvenator, and he is also the One who goes before in creating and exemplifying environments that respect and cultivate beauty and healthy, sustainable rhythms.

These express humanity as God intended – with ebb and flow, engagement and disengagement as part and parcel to our development as Christ-ians (or "little Christs," as C.S. Lewis labeled us). We are in a secondary sense instruments designed to achieve God's grand purposes; we are, however, primarily his children who are called to be as much as to do. If plants get the order screwed up, it can lead to burn out, unsustainable growth, and discipleship as a performance treadmill. Living as a "contrast society," as Alan Roxburgh describes the Church's call in culture, means that we ultimately live into hard ministry among the margins, while at the same time we live out a narrative that is full-orbed, life-giving, and relevant across diverse societal strata. This holism is essentially the expression of what's meant by a communal call to live holistically as a sign and foretaste of God's shalom order that is now and yet coming.

Superficial Theological Roots and Connections to Praxis

"Missional" has become a word that means everything ... and nothing. It has become a label to justify any outward stance in culture, rather than an intrinsic change in the way we live and operate as the people of God in the world. So much church planting is still governed by inherited, incomplete presuppositions about the gospel (individualized salvation and promise of glory), the state of the world (depraved), and the consummation of all things (usually involving a doing-away-with or a devaluing of life on earth in favor of an ethereal disembodied existence in "heaven") – to name a few. These work against creating new creation communities who demonstrate and proclaim another way to be human within the warp and woof of normal life on a bent earth. True missional church planters face the challenge of discerning how to start communities that are "in but not of" the world, rather than projecting themselves as "against and not of" or "outside and not of" the world (like too many new churches).

Weakness in Delegation or Need for Power

Team leaders who don't know how to delegate or who make others overly dependent on them as the center point of power, influence, communication and visibility will run into problems and create problems. Taking risks in developing and empowering other leaders is absolutely essential for team and church health. I'm a firm believer in what some have called "revolving power," which doesn't negate point leadership and responsibility but defers leadership of key areas and stages of a plant to those gifted to best lead those. The inability to delegate isn't necessarily a character issue and can be counteracted through training. However, needing to be the center of it all definitely is a character issue that will eventually become problematic. This relates to the next challenge.

Maturity and/or "dark side" issues

Points of immaturity or hidden and unaddressed character flaws in the core leader (or among his/her team) often emerge under the pressure of planting. It is not uncommon for leaders to respond well to the urgencies ever besetting their plant, all the while not giving much time at all to their own leadership development and accountability. All leaders have areas of weakness and brokenness as well as blindsides, and these must be brought into self-awareness and addressed intentionally. Planters are often surprised or even shocked to discover the muck that comes up in themselves in the cauldron of church start-ups. What is critical, of course, is how a leader responds to what emerges. When a church planting team gets derailed or waylaid because the primary leader is confronted with developmental issues, the project's success may hinge on whether the leader can exhibit proper humility and a willingness to seek help. Problems or hindering issues in the lives of leaders are often due to their own chosen isolation. This means that mentors, meaningful peer relationships, and even therapists must be cultivated as safety nets. When leaders do confess sin and humbly acknowledge their need for help, this stance often works wonders to get teams that have been damaged by poor or compromised leadership back on track.

Moving Too Quickly to a [usually Sunday] Public Gathering

Church planting according to the church growth school is too often more about launching a public service than planting a church that's able to equip existing and new disciples of Jesus. Plant leaders will need to resist the urge to give too much energy and visibility to a weekly central gathering. (Christians with kids who are part of the core, by the way, will often push team leaders to meet and service their children somehow, thinking that a Sunday gig is the best mode for this. That's why it's good to have a plan that invites parents into seeking a better solution.) Once a leadership team has established a centralized gathering as the *center of gravity* for the plant (note the italicized phrase!), it is very hard if nearly impossible to go back and recreate a healthy balance between the church's gathered and scattered expressions. Before "throwing the doors open" for all who will come (i.e., "churching together"), leaders must themselves come to harmony on their identity and what matters most (i.e., their values) to the forming community. Even more importantly, they must actually identify and begin practicing a way of life together (discipleship) BEFORE they make the forming church too permeable to others beyond the core. In other words, the leadership team cannot broker others into a Jesus way of life (discipleship pattern) that they themselves have not taken the time to rehearse together. If a plant team and their core have not done the work in clarifying vision, identity, values and way of life (i.e., core practices) before visibly "churching," they will be subject to the whims and agendas of every Christian coming into their midst (this relates to the next challenge). This DNA piece that comes from rehearsing their desired identity and discipleship pattern is vital, but it does not preclude gathering as a substantial expression of body life. Centralized gatherings are not to be avoided, as long as leaders do not weight the "come to us" dynamic so much that they both damage discipleship and also extract people from their natural interface with the world Jesus wants them "in, but not of."

Incoming disenfranchised or "churchy-land" Christians

In any city there are disgruntled or floating unattached Christians who are looking for a better church experience or simply a church that fits their preferences. Plants have to beware of the consumers or church hoppers looking for greener ecclesial pastures. An influx of transfers and/or floaters can bog down a plant. We're all socialized into certain ways of being Christians by the church cultures we come out of (this is what I mean by "churchy-land" culture), so it's important to recognize that some healthy deprogramming and reinfusion of new DNA needs to happen among all those coming into the core community of a plant (NOTE: Every church will have a culture emerge, and I'm not suggesting that's bad. Followers of Christ need to be socialized into a countercultural way of life where certain mainstream cultural narratives must be resisted – consumerism, busyness, individualism, etc. What we need deprogramming from are "extractionist" churchy behaviors that make us appear unnecessarily religious eggheads to normal people.) Planters need to be careful not to make it too easy for floating Christians to belong, as they'll eventually discover clashes of values and even hidden agendas. Toward that end it's advisable to institute some kind of debriefing process among the lead team, which should include exploring how an incoming Christian closed off with the church he/she just left or previously belonged to.

Lack of Communal Discernment Processes or a Listening Posture

If planters cannot hear God and apply wisdom in setting priorities on what the team and core should and should not take on, this becomes a recipe for burnout or being subject to the proverbial tyranny of the urgent (or at minimum, vision dispersion and overreach). Many planters are naturally restless activists and visionaries, which is part of what's needed to get new things started. But if they can't embrace the value of creating spaces and paces conducive to hearing (for themselves individually and for their teams communally), they're treading dangerously into the zone of scattered, potentially low yield, hyperactivity.

Anti-organizational Bias or Anti-Tradition

I'm maybe cheating by blending two challenges into one. At times some planters extol only organic, more liquid forms of church as best, when this unfairly and unwisely disregards both the spirituality of good organizational development and also the learnings and depth of more traditional churches. This denial of some beneficial good from what has gone before is at times expressed in leaders being overly mesmerized with the latest and greatest ideas. It's important to note that all healthy organic entities have a maturing organizational framework; that's to be expected as long as it serves the body's development.

There's another related issue worth mentioning: being overly progressive. This can mean that a leader becomes too idealistic and unable to assimilate concrete, mid-to-late adopters. Such folks can become the backbone of a healthy church, but only if they are valued enough by leadership who must do extra work to help such disciples understand what it is the plant is trying to do and why. Some planters also resist the idea of good planning, relegating that to the realm of the "unspiritual" (i.e., it's too much of a pain in the neck to waste time with). Without some degree of organizational savvy and forward planning, which includes the capacity to develop some early systems for equipping, communication, assimilation, people development, etc., a plant will remain dangling (often precariously) on the edge of sustainability.

Social base issues – Inadequate Regard for Critical Support Systems

Preserving a healthy social base more often than not includes lending adequate time and attention to one's spouse and children. The issue of harmony over the lead planter's call to church plant is extremely important, as many a plant goes down because a leader gets too far ahead of his/her spouse or family needs. Church planting can become nearly all-consuming, at least in certain patches. So leaders definitely need to have their spouse/family on board, at least having them agree to be supportive and not antagonistic to the idea of planting. Having said that, planters do need to be good at setting boundaries to protect the intrusion of "ministry" into every sphere of their lives. Of course, social base also applies to leaders who are single. The preservation of close supportive relationships, and a home/leisure life that allows some respite from the stresses of planting is important for single and married planters alike.

About Dan Stiegerwald

Dan Steigerwald resides in SE Portland with his wife Ann, and daughters Andrea and Jenn. Prior to arriving in Portland in 2006, the Steigerwalds served 18 years in Holland as missionaries, church-planters and project coaches. Dan serves as Christian Associate's (CA) North America Director. He holds a Doctor of Ministry in Leadership in the Emerging Culture from George Fox Seminary. Ann is originally from Canada, and has recently taken on the HR leadership role for CA. The Steigerwalds are passionate about sustainable living practices that honor God and His creation while promoting good stewardship.

Afterword

Re-learning Evangelicalism in Post-Christendom
Scott Hagley

In the end, conferences, theories, and expert opinion only carry us so far. Eventually, we must venture into risky terrain and find our way. We learn through risk and reflection. A few months ago I was at the community pool with my daughters for a Friday night "loonie swim." They decided it was time to learn how to flip from the side into the pool. My oldest daughter (age 8) tends to approach new situations like a theorist. She consulted with me on the mechanics of the flip, correlating her observations with the instructions that I gave her. After a few minutes of observation and reflection, we began to sketch a theory of the flip: she should jump high and outward, tuck her head and make sure that her legs rotate. But we never finished the sketch. Mid-sentence, the body of my youngest daughter (age 7) barreled over us and splashed into the pool in a near-perfect flip. My youngest daughter tends to approach new situations as a mystic. She did not want to talk about the flip, but wanted to experience it firsthand. It was only after several attempts at the flip that she was open to reflection and conversation about it. In the end, both girls learned something new in practice and understanding. My oldest wanted to establish language and frameworks first while my youngest needed experimental experience so that she could understand instruction and perfect the skill.

Something like this moment is captured in *Text & Context*. While discovery requires both risk and reflection, the post-Christendom conversation has been dominated by shifts in language and frameworks. These shifts have been so successful that theologians and pastors across Canada use the language of post-Christendom. We largely understand ourselves as living in a new kind of era. But this acknowledgment remains incomplete on its own. Naming our location leads to another question: What does the life of the evangelical church look like in post-Christendom Canada? In response to this question, we need the risk-takers and mystics, the pragmatists and those hungry for experience. Discovery requires real-world risk.

Text & Context demonstrates just this kind of learning. In these essays, we encounter firsthand accounts of missional experimentation with the added benefit of theological reflection. While some church plants, such as Saint Benedict's Table in Winnipeg, begin by reflecting missiologically on their own tradition and shape practices accordingly, others, such as Little Flowers (also in Winnipeg), establish rhythms of formation and mission before their theological work reveals that they are, in fact, a church. Intentional reflection on text and context leads to engagement and risk while our experiences of risk and engagement compel us to make sense of what happened. Both approaches lead us into faithful church practice in post-Christendom. I give thanks for the risk-takers and innovators in this book.

But what are we learning from the previous essays? On the surface, we encounter a disparate set of stories about church planting at a particular time in Canada. While this is interesting on its own, I want to suggest that these missional experiments offer an important sense of direction regarding the future of evangelicalism in post-Christendom Canada. In recent years it has become evident that the loss of Christendom has particular implications for North American evangelicalism. An evangelical self-understanding rooted in the Great Awakening (what Douglas Sweeney calls the evangelical "eighteenth-century twist") now encounters an increasingly pluralist public sphere where Christian language and calls for conversion struggle for plausibility. Persons across the evangelical spectrum have recognized this challenge and struggled to find an appropriate response. In these essays, we see the re-shaping of evangelical identity through an emphasis on *formation* before *proclamation.* It seems that the loss of a generic theistic or Christian consensus in society necessitates distinct communities of practice where Christian language can be taught and Christian truth proclaimed. While this is not stated directly, nearly every church-plant in this book begins with a description of its formational practices. The days of "if you build it, [they] will come" are over. In what follows, I will describe the present identity crisis for North American evangelicalism and draw upon several *Text & Context* essays in order to articulate features of a renewed post-Christendom evangelicalism. We may be in the midst of a twenty-first century evangelical metamorphosis.

Evangelicalism in Christendom

It should not be surprising that evangelicalism struggles with a sense of identity. Indeed, the movement seems to slip away from any attempts at definition. Some of the most generally accepted approaches, such as David Bebbington's quadrilateral, try to describe evangelicals through categories of shared belief and emphasis in practice.[1] But the diversity of theological traditions that make up modern evangelicalism means that descriptions of shared belief and practice like Bebbington's are often too generic to say anything distinctive about evangelicalism. That is, they fail to articulate *positively* what makes an evangelical different from, say, a committed Lutheran. Others, such as George Marsden and Ernest Sandeen understand evangelicalism in terms of its historical progression from the fundamentalist movement at the turn of the twentieth century.[2] This approach has the added advantage of including specific theological commitments shared by most evangelicals within a broader historical, political, and social context. But not all contemporary evangelicals can trace their roots to fundamentalism and some of the break-away groups from that era. Modern evangelicalism remains a trans-denominational movement where certain Anglicans can share an ethos with Baptists or Nazarenes. Still others see evangelicalism as a "kaleidoscope" of diversity and resign themselves to partial descriptions and historical context rather than firm definitions.[3]

In the midst of these approaches, Douglas Sweeney provides a concise and workable definition that works well for our task today. Sweeney states that evangelicalism is: "a movement of orthodox Protestants with an eighteenth-century twist."[4] Sweeney's definition clarifies several things. First, he draws attention to its intrinsic diversity as a movement rather than an organization or a denomination. One participates within evangelicalism by choice rather than association. Second, evangelicals affirm an understanding of the gospel rooted in the Reformation. Primarily this is expressed in evangelical fervor for the Scriptures and an articulation of salvation by faith. This is Sweeney's attempt to outline the basics of evangelical belief. But there are lots of movements characterized by an orthodox Protestant belief. What is it that makes evangelicals different from other such groups? Sweeney argues that it is the "eighteenth-century twist" that is our evangelical legacy.

Sweeney's term "eighteenth-century twist" refers, of course, to the Great Awakening, a trans-Atlantic religious renewal generated by figures as distinct as John and Charles Wesley, George Whitfield, and Jonathan Edwards. As such, the movement drew upon Puritan, Anglican, and Pietist roots and featured both a call to conversion (or perhaps recommitment) as well as a seriousness regarding discipleship. Although the Reformed theology of Edwards remained distinct from the more Arminian flavour of Wesley, the Awakening insisted upon the personal commitment or response of faith *alongside* or *accompanied by* authentic religious experience.

Like the Pietists and Puritans of earlier eras, the Awakening(s) rejected theology as a scholastic enterprise and understood it as an act of devotion.[5] This opened the door to more subjective and experiential accounts of faith, as the account of salvation thickened from an objective participation in the sacramental life of the church to include subjective accounts of experience. Even the theological sophistication of Jonathan Edwards was engaged in studious reflection on the experiences and stories of revival, keeping theology and religious affection together.[6]

These are the best features of our legacy: an insistence on salvation by faith through grace that takes seriously affective religious experience and disciplined discipleship.

But we must also recognize that this legacy has fallen on tough times, for these eighteenth-century shifts in theology and the importance of experience must be understood within the framework of Christendom, where religious participation was linked to both geography and national identity. The Awakening(s) insisted upon personal responses of faith within a context where most people had experience with baptism and participation in the sacraments. Evangelicals insisted that it was not enough to be baptized and to take the Eucharist, we must *respond* to the gospel in faith and have a subsequent *experience* of religious enlightenment. Of course, these themes have always been present in the Church in one form or another. But the Awakening(s) present a unique emergence of these themes in several places and in several different ecclesial traditions at the same time.

From the First Great Awakening to Billy Graham revivals, from the Fundamentalist-Modernist split to the reign of "seeker-sensitive" churches, evangelical faith and self-understanding have taken place within and often *because of* a Christendom context. In the great awakening, Puritan and Pietist traditions blended to preach a personal experience of conversion and practices of personal piety to those who were *already* church members. They insisted that the Christian life is something *more* than baptism, Eucharist, and nominal church attendance within the confines of Christendom.[7] The faith needs to be made personal. Or, put differently, the faith is not only a work that happens to us, but one that requires our full individual commitment and participation. In more recent times, folks like Billy Graham have popularized the question "Have you made Jesus your personal Lord and Saviour?" both to talk about Jesus' life and work and to invite others into a life of faith. By placing renewed emphasis on the personal and experiential elements of faith, this "eighteenth-century twist" minimized the more social, traditional, and habitual elements of faith formation.[8] In some ways, the personal decision of an individual believer pushed the formative practices of Christ's body into the background.

Loss and Re-Learning: Evangelicalism in Post-Christendom

We can see these emphases still present in evangelicalism today. The emphasis on personal experience and responsibility resonates across the denominational spectrum, while evangelicals remain cautious with both academic theology and any emphasis on objective sacramental participation. But something significant has changed which makes evangelicalism's eighteenth- century twist problematic: the dramatic foil for evangelical relevance—Christendom—has crumbled. We have fewer opportunities to call those with a casual relationship to

Christianity into a more intentional faith. In the post-Christendom landscape, we now find ourselves struggling to fill the institutional and ecclesial gaps left by Christendom. The loss of Christendom also translates into a loss for evangelicalism.

One can observe this crisis within the spectrum of "neo's" that now populate the evangelical landscape. Neo-Reformed leaders have grabbed onto the Reformed strands of the evangelical story and doubled-down on them, insisting upon a fairly rigid application of historical Calvinism. These groups have responded to the loss of intelligibility by tightening the boundaries of Christian orthodoxy to specific propositions. While this has brought a sense of cohesion to those within the movement, its insistence on a propositional faith has excluded the more Pietist and experiential forms of evangelicalism. Others, such as emergent, neo-evangelical, or even those who call themselves post-evangelical have taken the opposite tack. In the face of a fragmentary evangelical identity, they have insisted upon the priority of personal experience grounded within the ancient traditions and practices of the Church. Like the neo-Reformed, they also attach evangelicalism to something rooted and grounded, though it is in particular practices rather than particular doctrines.

Both approaches, however, have been found wanting. Both leave behind some part of the evangelical legacy. Both, in the end, tend to overcome the loss of Christendom by reconstituting the categories of Christendom. But *Text & Context* provides evidence that apart from the bulk of books and conferences dotting the evangelical landscape, a new expression of evangelicalism is taking root that retains its "eighteenth-century twist" while adding, perhaps, a twenty-first century metamorphosis. As evangelicals have lost supporting social structures that make proclamation plausible, we see a promising shift toward practices of formation rooted in a more social understanding of the gospel and a practical engagement with Christian tradition.

First, we see in these chapters a shift from a gospel of personal commitment to one that recognizes the unavoidable social dimensions of such a commitment. For example, in Robert Cameron's portrayal of Downtown Windsor Community Cooperative (DWCC) (ch. 4), Cameron assumes that "the community modeled in the middle of the everyday life of the neighbourhood is the greatest apologetic for the gospel." This is a phrase that calls to mind Paul's "only let your manner of life together be worthy of the gospel" in Philippians 1:27, for it seeks to understand the way in which a community can demonstrate the good news of Jesus Christ. In such a framework, the gospel is not only a call to individual commitment, but a participation in a gospel-ed people. In Christendom, evangelicals were caught between fundamentalist and "social gospel" commitments, which chastened the social implications of the gospel. We found ourselves choosing between personal moral purity--don't drink, don't smoke—or a commitment to particular images of economic justice. But as the DWCC seeks to live as good news in the neighbourhood, something different takes place. It is not just that the gospel carries a particular set of social commitments, but that one's social context shapes the very expression and understanding of the gospel.

Cameron tells us that DWCC does its theological reflection within the struggles, hopes, and questions of the neighbourhood: What would it look like if God moved into *this* place? And how do we join? The result for DWCC is a collaborative life, where the personal commitment demanded by the gospel is inseparable from a *people* with whom we commit and a *place* where we live out this commitment. The eighteenth-century twist takes on a new shape. This shift in practice may not have found adequate ecclesiological language, but this certainly looks like the makings of a robust and evangelical ecclesiology: the church as a cooperative people of the way.[9]

Second, we see a renewed interest on the part of evangelicals in the riches of their own traditions for the sake of mission and discipleship. This follows directly from a more social understanding of the gospel. In my experience, evangelicals tend to be either resistant or romantic toward the idea of tradition. On the one hand, the revivalist strands of evangelicalism play tradition over and against a vibrant, personal encounter with Jesus. This has made evangelical forms of worship, church organization, and ministry adaptive and innovative. But it has also made our collective memory short, and it has authorized attempts to restore the first century without accounting for the twenty centuries in-between. Our thin appropriation of history invites criticism and creates its own backlash where evangelicals in recent years have sought a romantic and individualized return to Christian tradition. While we can celebrate a renewed interest in monasticism or contemplative worship, such a return to tradition remains tethered to an individualist version of the gospel. It is still the individual who appropriates or selectively engages tradition on his or her own terms.

But we see something different in these pages. Here, several church planters have resisted the temptation to engage a generic and selective church tradition while exploring the contours of their own particular tradition and history for the sake of mission and discipleship. In both Jamie Howison's (ch. 10) Saint Benedict's Table and Frank Emanuel's Freedom Vineyard (ch. 5), an attempt is made to stand within and under a particular strand of the Christian wisdom for the sake of formation. An intentional appeal to ancient spiritual practices, to historically-conscious liturgies and self-understanding helps both Howison and Emanuel solve particular problems around the formation of Christian character and community. They do not call individuals to select which parts of the tradition fit them, but rather intend to shape the community in worship and spiritual formation through the resources and practices of their particular strand of historical Christianity.

Their intentional and disciplined engagement with tradition is crucial for our time. When evangelicalism was a renewal movement within Christendom, such work was not as pressing. Evangelism and discipleship took place in a culturally-coherent environment. Persons came to faith already formed in a theistic or perhaps generically Christian framework. Discipleship could focus on individual resources like a "choose your own adventure" story. But this is no longer a practical or effective way of shaping disciples because of the social fragmentation that has accompanied the loss of Christendom. Persons now come to the faith and even the church shaped by a bewildering variety of stories and practices. Our Christian identity rests uneasily within this fragmentary matrix.

Here Howison and Emmanuel—as well as others in this volume— approach this problem with a pragmatic, problem-solving perspective. That is, they approach it with the same innovation and can-do activism of previous generations of evangelicals. They do not call us back to a romanticized vision of a traditional faith, nor do they form a rigid ideology. Rather, they return to their respective historical roots in search of wisdom and they experiment with ways of life that form a counter-cultural people, that create communities of discipleship rather than individualized resources for discipleship.

213

Conclusion

In zoology, metamorphosis names the transition or transformation of a creature from one form of life to another. It is a remarkable part of maturation and survival for certain species that involves both continuity and discontinuity. It is a picture in the natural world of the way in which disruption can bring about something new, surprising, and life-giving. I wonder if we are seeing signs of renewal and innovation in post-Christendom evangelicalism, an innovation that comes to us first in practice and risk before we can find adequate language and theological clarity. Theologians across Canada will do well to pay attention and come alongside these missional communities so that we might clarify and nurture a twenty-first century evangelicalism in the name and hope of Christ.

About Scott Hagley

Scott Hagley, Ph.D. Luther Seminary, is a teaching pastor at Southside Community Church and the Director of Education for Forge Canada. Before coming to Southside and Forge, Scott worked as a researcher and church consultant for Church Innovations Institute and taught courses in theology, mission, and leadership at Bethel University, Rochester College, and Augsburg College. Scott lives in proximity with Southside in a culturally-diverse neighbourhood of Vancouver, BC, with his wife and two daughters.

Bibliography

Balmer, Randall Herbert. *Blessed Assurance: A History of Evangelicalism in America*. Boston: Beacon, 1999.

Bebbington, D.W. *Evangelicalism in Modern Britain: A History from the 1730s to the 1980s*. Boston: Unwin Hyman, 1989.

Marsden, George M. *Fundamentalism and American Culture*. 2nd ed. New York: Oxford University Press, 2006.

Noll, Mark A. *The Rise of Evangelicalism: The Age of Edwards, Whitefield, and the Wesleys*, A History of Evangelicalism Vol. 1. Downers Grove: InterVarsity, 2003.

Olson, Roger E. "Free Church Ecclesiology and Evangelical Spirituality." In *Evangelical Ecclesiology: Reality or Illusion?*, edited by John Gordon Stackhouse, 161-78. Grand Rapids: Baker Academic, 2003.

Sandeen, Ernest Robert. *The Roots of Fundamentalism: British and American Millenarianism, 1800-1930*. Chicago: University of Chicago Press, 1970.

Smith, Timothy L. "The Evangelical Kaleidoscope and the Call the Christian Unity." *Christian Scholar's Review* 15:2 (1986) 125-40.

Sweeney, Douglas A. *The American Evangelical Story: A History of the Movement*. Grand Rapids: Baker Academic, 2005.

---

1 Bebbington describes the quadrilateral of evangelical priorities: "*conversionism*, the belief that lives need to be changed; *activism*, the expression of the gospel in effort; *biblicism*, a particular regard for the Bible; and what may be called *crucicentrism*, a stress on the sacrifice of Christ on the cross." See Bebbington, *Evangelicalism in Modern Britain: A History from the 1730s to the 1980s*, 3.

2 Sandeen understands evangelicalism in relationship to millennialism. Marsden understands modern evangelicals as more worldly-minded heirs of the fundamentalist movement. See Sandeen, *The Roots of Fundamentalism: British and American Millenarianism, 1800-1930*. See also Marsden, *Fundamentalism and American Culture*.

3 This is a position held by scholars like Randall Balmer and Timothy L. Smith. See Randall Herbert Balmer, *Blessed Assurance: A History of Evangelicalism in America*. See also Timothy L. Smith, "The Evangelical Kaleidoscope and the Call the Christian Unity," *Christian Scholar's Review* 15:2 (1986).

4 Sweeney, *The American Evangelical Story: A History of the Movement*, 24.

5 Space demands that I leave these two movements uncomfortably side-by-side. The fact that they both influence evangelicalism is perhaps part of what makes the movement so difficult to define. Roger Olson insists that the Pietist/experiential and Puritan/orthodox Protestant traditions provide a kind of "bipolar" center. See Roger E. Olson, "Free Church Ecclesiology and Evangelical Spirituality," in *Evangelical Ecclesiology: Reality or Illusion?*, ed. John Gordon Stackhouse.

6 We can see this in Edwards' own work, such as his *A Treatise Concerning Religious Affections* (1746), where he is concerned with a serious theological account of religious experience.

7 The overriding evangelical concern was - and it could be argued still *is* - "a commitment to the ideal and the practice of a genuine Christianity" which was found in changed selves or in "fashioning spiritual communities in which changed selves could grow in grace." See Mark A. Noll, *The Rise of Evangelicalism: The Age of Edwards, Whitefield, and the Wesleys, A History of Evangelicalism Vol. 1.*, 262.

8 Roger Olson calls this emphasis on the individual response of faith "conversional piety." Olson, "Free Church Ecclesiology and Evangelical Spirituality," 165.

9 In this vein, see also Laurence East and Metro Community Church in Kelowna (ch. 9).

About the Editor

Len Hjalmarson lives with his wife Betty on the shores of lake Superior in Thunder Bay, Ontario where they help to lead a faith community on a journey in mission.

Len is co-author of *Missional Spirituality* (IVP: 2011), and author of *The Missional Church Fieldbook* (Urban Loft, 2012). His next book, *No Home Like Place: A Christian Theology of Place* will appear in 2014.

Len is a member of the Parish Collective, and an adjunct professor at Northern Baptist Theological Seminary in Chicago, at Tyndale Seminary, Toronto and George Fox Evangelical Seminary in Portland. He loves good music, good books, and good cooking.

About ULP

Urban Loft Publishers focuses on ideas, topics, themes, and conversations about all things urban. Renewing the city is the central theme and focus of what we publish. It is our intention to blend urban ministry, theology, urban planning, architecture, urbanism, stories, and the social sciences, as ways to drive the conversation. While we lean heavily towards scholarly and academic works, we explore the fun and lighter sides of cities as well. We publish a wide variety of urban perspectives, from books by the experts about the city to personal stories and personal accounts of urbanites who live in the city.

Other Books by ULP

The Missional Church Fieldbook
Leonard Hjalmarson

Paperback: $14.99; Kindle: $7.99.

Tools for helping believers transition into missional practices have been absent or rare: until now. *The Missional Church Fieldbook* is a tool for use in groups to transition from inward to outward focus, and to work together to discover shared disciplines of mission and community. *The Missional Church Fieldbook* will require that you ... move from the life of a member to a missionary ... begin a journey to an unknown destination ... open your life deeply to at least three other people ... recognize that you are God's possession and inheritance ... reimagine your life within God's big story ... discover a messy spirituality ... get outside your comfort zone.

"*The Missional Church Fieldbook* is an excellent resource for communities of faith who want to be intentional in embracing and developing a missional orientation in both heart and mind. With an excellent rhythm of individual and communal reflection around the primary truths of God's mission, this fieldbook puts missional in the hands of the people at a time when the term missional has begun to be deeply misunderstood. It will bring willing people back to the heart of God and in community with one another." -- **Shelley Campagnola**, Heritage Seminary, Cambridge, ON

They're Just Not That Into You:
The Church's Struggle for Relevancy in the 21st Century
Stephen R. Harper

Paperback: $5.99; Kindle: $2.99.

Close to 90% of Canadians say they still believe in God, yet less than 15% go to church on a regular basis. Why is there such a disconnect between church and culture? *They're Just Not That Into You: The Church's Search for Relevancy in the 21st Century* explores this question. Author Stephen Harper delves into the curious shift that has occurred in western society, studying the cultural nuances affecting the church's ability to significantly influence the world around it. So is there a solution? *They're Just Not That Into You* investigates this reality and offers some practical solutions.

"Through rich theological reflection, sociological evaluation, scientific survey and sharing the stories of rooted Christian communities, Stephen Harper offers the Canadian - and global - church a valuable resource for engaging and adapting our faith practices for the advance of the *missio dei* in our post-modern, pluralistic realities. We need churches who are willing to release their agenda's in submission to the work Jesus desires to do in the lives of the individuals and communities we have been called. Harper's work and experience offers a framework through which to do just that." -- **Jon Huckins** is on staff with NieuCommunities, is the Co-Founder of The Global Immersion Project & author of *Thin Places & Teaching Through the Art of Storytelling.*

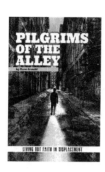

Pilgrims of the Alley:
Living Out Faith in Displacement
Dave Arnold

Paperback: $11.99; Kindle: $7.99.

Sometimes people wonder why they feel stuck in life, as if they are living out their days in an unnatural and often hostile environment. But the truth is, this is a reality for people attempting to follow Jesus in our world. We are displaced persons. But God is at work in displacement. And it's in this environment – in the alleys of life – where extraordinary growth takes place and our faith grows the most. This book is about a journey of understanding how we are to navigate a life of faith amid a world of such uncertainty, and oftentimes, of great darkness.

"*Pilgrims of the Alley* gives me hope of things to come. Dave writes with a profound purpose and reflects the light of a loving God calling his people home." -- **Justin Zoradi**, Founder of These Numbers Have Faces and JustinZoradi.com.

"I was reminded and encouraged that living out our love for Christ as aliens in this land is essential for an authentic and vibrant faith in our broken world." -- **Noel Castellanos**, CEO, Christian Community Development Association.

Made in the USA
Middletown, DE
17 April 2016